The Field Sales Handbook

JIM COWDEN

the Institute of Management

FOUNDATION

PITMAN PUBLISHING

PITMAN PUBLISHING
128 Long Acre, London WC2E 9AN

A Division of Longman Group Limited

First published in Great Britain 1994

© Jim Cowden 1994

A CIP catalogue record for this book can be obtained
from the British Library

ISBN 0 273 60716 2

1 3 5 7 9 10 8 6 4 2

Photoset in Century Schoolbook by
Northern Phototypesetting Co. Ltd., Bolton
Printed and bound in Great Britain
by Bell and Bain Ltd, Glasgow

*The Publishers' policy is to use paper manufactured
from sustainable forests.*

Contents

■

Introduction   vii

1 WHERE TO BEGIN   1

2 QUALITY OF ACTIVITY   24

3 IDENTIFYING THE DIRECTION OF ACTIVITY   47

4 HOW TO GET FACE TO FACE   83

5 EFFICIENT WORKING IN THE FIELD   109

6 SOME SPECIAL SITUATIONS   127

7 LET'S TALK ABOUT NEGOTIATING   153

8 CONSOLIDATING YOUR POSITION AND SECURING
  YOUR FUTURE   169

  Conclusion   203

  Bibliography   205

  Index   206

Introduction

■

There must have been hundreds of excuses invented by sales people to explain why they failed to sell to customers, or why they didn't achieve their targets or objectives and, in some cases, why they didn't even manage to make enough appointments to see the customers in the first place. I say there must be hundreds, because I have used at least as many as that, having either picked them up from other sales people, or been fairly creative in inventing a few new ones of my own.

The problem with this book is that there should be a bold **Health Warning** on the front cover:

> **IF YOU LET YOUR SALES MANAGER READ THIS BOOK, YOU WILL HAVE SAID GOOD-BYE TO ALL THE EXCUSES YOU WERE EVER ABLE TO USE.**

I have set the book out in sections which address the most common problems that sales people encounter:

- First, the **quantity** of your **activity**
  - the physical number of calls you need to get through in order to produce the results.

- Second, the **quality** of your **activity**
  - how well and successfully you carry out those calls.

- Third, the **direction** of your **activity**
  - how to identify priorities to make sure that you are directing your activity in the right areas.

I once heard a splendid description of the difference between *efficient* and *effective* – Efficient is about *doing things properly*, whereas effective is about *doing the proper things*. I have spent many years in sales and management watching many people doing things with great efficiency, the only problem being that most of these were the wrong things.

Direction of activity is about being effective, efficiency we will address later in the book when you have learned how to be effective.

All of these topics will be covered in the section of the book where I introduce you to **'mapping the business'**, arguably the most powerful management concept in use in sales and management today, yet one of the simplest.

Recently I was working with sales people from Digital Equipment Corporation, one of the world's largest computer companies, when I introduced them to *mapping the business*. This was a fairly sophisticated and experienced group, so in my introduction I pointed out that within the concept, there really wasn't anything new, only a different and more structured way to plan your sales activity. At the end of the session, their manager stood up to thank me for the work I had done during the course of that day and commented on my remarks, *'It's only nothing new if you've seen it before, and no-one in this room has'*. So perhaps there are occasions when even I sell myself short. What I do know is that when you come to terms with the concept and continue to use it, you will become very successful and you will lead a much less stressful life.

Some of the other areas which I have included in this book are:

- How to make appointments so that you get face to face with customers.

- Some of the hi-tech solutions which are available to you today to help you run the business more efficiently.

- How to handle the particular problems associated with working from home.

I will also be looking at some of the **special situations** which confront sales people, like *selling to groups,* and that ever present problem that sales managers and directors hand down to us; How to *negotiate* when you haven't been given either the *training* or the *authority t*o do so.

Towards the end of the book, I will give you some ideas related to using letters and proposals to represent you in your absence, when it becomes much easier for the customer to make a negative decision, because you aren't there to handle objections and clarify understanding.

Finally, to help you build a more secure and successful career for yourself, I will give you a format for creating your own **personal development plan** (PDP), together with some thoughts on career development.

Throughout the book, however, I want you to adopt the KISS principle;

KISS = 'Keep It Simple, Stupid'.

I would like you to work through the book with me and I ask that knowing that the vast majority of sales people hate paperwork and in fact many of you hate work, period. It's one of the reasons we are in the profession, we simply want to be in front of our customers, telling our stories and getting the business.

A little time spent now will lay the foundations of a very successful business and career, so bear with me.

The other endearing quality that I find in sales people is their impatience. It's one of the reasons that companies hire us, we're not interested in what might happen tomorrow, we want it now and we become extremely creative in finding ways of making it happen **now**. But, as you work through this book I counsel you to be patient and it will work to your advantage.

Try to remember the parable of the old bull and the young bull:

An old bull and a young bull were overlooking a meadow in which there were about 30 cows grazing.

The young bull said, '*Let's gallop down there* and service some of those cows'.

Whereupon the old bull said, '*Let's just take our time* and we'll service them all'.

So as you work through this book, try to adopt the 'old bull' type of patience.

Actually, those of you who know me will not be surprised to learn that it took me longer to find the word 'service' as a printable alternative to the expressions I normally use, than it did to write the rest of this introduction!

As you go through the book try to bear in mind that within these pages I have tried to put together the contents of around six days of classroom training on one of my courses, so take your time and it will all come together.

Wherever you are, keep this book with you and use it as your professional 'Bible', but also keep this thought in the forefront of your mind;

If you apply last year's *quantity, quality* and *direction of activity* to this year's business, the best you can hope for is **last year's result** - and for most of us that will not be good enough.

Before I leave this introduction and move on to the main content of the book, I would like to thank my good friend Frank Munro, the well known and highly respected Glasgow optometrist, for pointing out to me that although this book has been written for sales people and sales managers, most of the content will be invaluable to anyone who manages his or her own business.

Where to begin

Identifying the necessary quantity of activity

TARGETS, BUDGETS AND FORECASTS

Typically what happens in most organisations is that shortly before the end of the current year, the sales management team hand down the **targets**, **budgets** or **forecasts** for the new year that, other than in exceptional circumstances, are simply the previous year's targets plus an increase of a few per cent.

They might just as well be using a crystal ball! Very seldom is any account taken of the state of the market – growing or declining, the actual achievement of the individual sales people during the previous year or the ability of the sales people to deliver the new targets. The most common situation is where the previous year's target was over-achieved and the actual achievement figure is taken – then increased. Where the target was under-achieved, the original target figure, which wasn't met, is taken and that figure is increased.

To improve your understanding of what follows, I would like to clarify my definitions for targets, budgets and forecasts – mainly because so many organisations use these words to describe different things:

- **Targets** are the financial and volume aims and objectives set for the sales force.

- **Budgets** represent the costs within which these targets will be achieved; e.g. salaries, commissions, cars, telephones etc.

- **Forecasts** are the results that the sales management team believe could be achieved – often higher than the targets that have been set, or they are the results that the sales force thinks it can produce.

Irrespective of my 'labels', please use the ones currently in force in your own company, which fit the definitions.

My experience has been that the owners or board of the company tell the sales management team what volume and financial objectives are needed or wanted for the new year, after which the sales managers redistribute these targets on a geographic basis, representing growth of sales in an area over the previous year.

Occasionally, this is broken down by the *product mix* which is preferred and the *customer mix* which is desired, but seldom is it made any more scientific than that.

There is a distinct process which should be followed and while a field sales force may be unable to exert any influence on a management team to follow this process, at least by understanding what it should be you will be able to highlight areas where you need help in achieving what often appears to be the unachievable.

Steps in securing the sales results

Step 1

On the basis of *quantifiable* **market research** or **market information**, the company must make decisions.

Most companies don't carry out any *real quality* market research. Indeed, some of the companies that I know who do carry out market research only do so with *retrospective* research, which tells them how successful they have been in the past few months or years.

As far as market information is concerned, many companies expect the sales force to provide *all* of this. It is true that the sales force can, and often do, provide some of this market information. However, the major problems associated with expecting sales people to provide all of this information are:

1 They don't have the time to carry out this function and also deliver the results.

2 They are not able to be objective in this area and in many cases that I have seen, the management team have been told what the sales force wanted them to know.

I think it's a bit like asking the fox to look after the chickens!

3 The sales force is neither qualified nor trained to carry out research which will provide *meaningful* information.

Finally, there is information available on the success rate of conducting market research in various markets which suggests the following:

Of 100 per cent of the companies being researched:

■ 5 per cent of the information on the companies being researched is out of date – therefore no real data is available.

■ 5 per cent of the companies being researched tell the researchers to GO AWAY!

Actually, the expression GO AWAY is seldom used, but neither Pitman Publishing nor The Institute of Management may be too pleased if I used the real-life expressions.

- 60 per cent of the companies researched have insufficient business available to justify any special effort.

- Only 30 per cent of the companies researched had sufficient business to place to warrant that special effort.

Before I fall foul of the market research organisations, I think that a 30 per cent return is extremely good, but not good enough to expect the sales force to carry this out and also deliver the goods.

Step 2

On the basis of real market information, the company should make **policy decisions** that, in detail, relate to the *total financial turnover, volume of goods*, the *product mix*, the *customer mix, profitability, market growth* and *geographic* circumstances etc.

Step 3

Analyse the results from each sales person in the previous year.

I could name you many companies, but had better not, who have taken last year's target, which may have been underachieved by 10 or 15 per cent, and increased it for the new year by a further 10per cent. The question I have to ask is, *'How the hell is the sales person going to achieve the new target when he or she was unable to deliver the old one?'*

Step 4

On the basis of the analysis, *new individual* targets should be set.

Step 5

Analyse the *quantity*, *quality* and *direction* of the activity that produced last year's result.

Step 6

Put in place a new and different **plan of action** in order to deliver the new target. Remember that last year's quantity, quality and direction of activity are extremely unlikely to deliver this year's result.

Step 7

Analyse the *qualifications* of the sales people being expected to provide the new activity and deliver the new targets, i.e. analyse the various areas of knowledge and skill.

Step 8

Put in place a **plan of development** to ensure that the sales people have the necessary qualifications to deliver the new plan of action.

The following flow chart – Figure 1.1 – will illustrate this concept more clearly.

When you look at the diagram you may not be surprised to learn that there is a school of thought which says that from Step 8 through Step 6 the process should be worked *backwards*, i.e. that there should be a constant process of development that should dictate what the plan of action should be.

While I have some sympathy for this idea, I prefer to look at Step 7 and Step 8 as giving you the ability to create a profile of the ideal sales person for the job.

From a management viewpoint, this is desirable for two reasons:

1 They know what needs to change in order to have their sales people fit the profile.
2 They have a profile of the replacement if the incumbent is unable or unwilling to change.

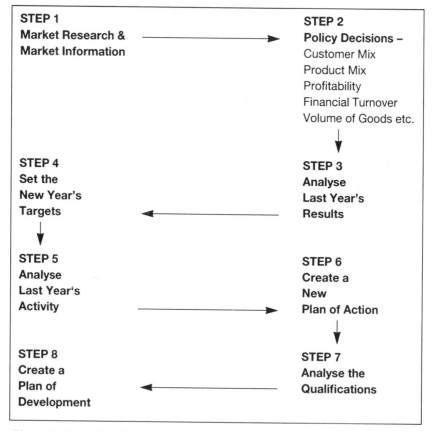

Fig. 1.1 Securing the sales results

The bottom line for the management team in any business that wishes to grow is:

> If you can't *change* the people – you have to change
> *the people!*

The Business MAP

We will return to this thinking after we have explored The Business MAP. MAP is an acronym for **Managing Activity and Productivity**.

Those of you who are familiar with my work will know that I place great emphasis on what I call 'word pictures'. I constantly refer to *mapping the business* because it creates a mental image of laying out and planning the future in much the same way that you would refer to a map when planning a journey, not unlike the 'journey' which is your career and your livelihood.

There are only three areas where you can get business:

1 Market opportunities;
2 Working opportunities;
3 Your existing customer base.

MARKET OPPORTUNITIES

These are prospects that you have identified, but you haven't yet contacted with regard to the opportunity to develop or create business.

They only become **market opportunities** when you have the name of the contact, his or her position (or their ability to influence) and you have an idea of the nature and perhaps even the size of the opportunity, i.e. *you have a valid reason for calling*.

Some time ago, I was running sales training with a group of direct sales people who were under contract to one of the largest insurance companies in the UK. When I came to the part of the programme where I introduced them to mapping

7

the business, I asked them to make a list of their market opportunities, whereupon several of them reached for the local telephone directory.

My view is that this may be one of the more basic ways of putting together a market research list, but a list of market opportunities it certainly wasn't. So I collected all of the telephone directories from them and promptly dropped them in the nearest waste paper basket, just to get the message across.

When you have made contact with regard to the opportunity and you have met to discuss this, and as a result of the meeting the prospect is still 'live', they become **working opportunities**.

WORKING OPPORTUNITIES

These are prospects on whom you are 'working' who have not yet made the decision to buy, in relation to the opportunity. When they make the decision to buy for the first time, they join your **existing customer base**.

When I take this thinking further, as we develop the *mapping concept*, I will fine tune this for you to help you to identify strategic considerations when dealing with these customers, but for the moment we'll regard them as being part of your existing customer base.

In line with my practice of creating mental images, I have always regarded my sales territory as the 'whole cake' from which I wanted to carve out my *'slice'*. With that in mind, the following diagram – Figure 1.2 – may help you understand the concept, particularly as we build this up together.

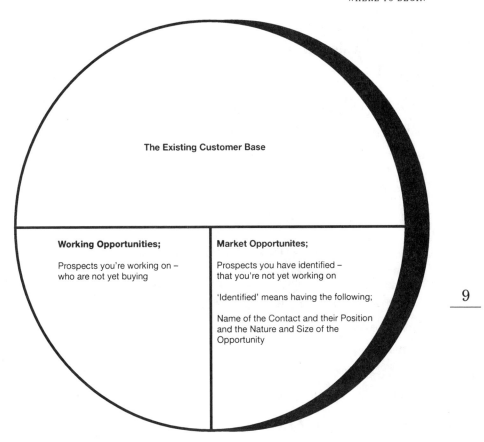

The Existing Customer Base

Working Opportunities;

Prospects you're working on –
who are not yet buying

Market Opportunites;

Prospects you have identified –
that you're not yet working on

'Identified' means having the following;

Name of the Contact and their Position
and the Nature and Size of the
Opportunity

Fig. 1.2 Mapping the business: the known market

Mapping the business

What I intend to do at this point is take you through the complete stages of mapping the business, after which I will refer back to various parts as we examine *quantity, quality* and *direction* of activity in greater detail.

LISTING YOUR CUSTOMERS

Having identified the three areas from where we can get business, I would now like you to split your existing customer base into three parts, the **regular buying customers**, the **core business** and the **infrequent buyers**.

Most of you will probably have some form of computer printout which lists your customers, but if you haven't, use Table 1.1 as an outline.

List all of your existing customer base, in order of importance, i.e. the *biggest value* customers first. Now go back over your list and by adding up the values of last year's business, or this year's forecast, if the change is significant, go through the list until you have marked the customers who are responsible for 80 per cent of your turnover.

These are your **core business** and should now be transferred to the Core business list which follows – see Table 1.2.

There is a rule in business which is known as the **'80/20' rule**; i.e. 80 per cent of your business will come from 20 per cent of your customers. The figure is not exact, it may come out at 75 per cent or even 85 per cent, but by and large I have found over the years that the '80/20' rule tends to hold up.

Later in this book when we look at how to approach your business strategically, you will find important differences between how you approach your *core business* and how you approach the other *regular buying customers*.

From the balance of your existing customer base list, identify those customers who buy from you *infrequently*.

Transfer these to the Infrequent buyers list which follows, see Table 1.3.

The remainder are your regular buying customers and should be transferred to the following list, see Table 1.4.

If we revisit the 'whole cake' diagram it should now look like Figure 1.3 (p. 15).

Table 1.1 The existing customer base

Customer & Contact	Last Year's Business	This Year's Forecast

Table 1.2 Core business

Customer & Contact	Last Year's Business	This Year's Forecast	Excess/ Shortfall to date

Table 1.3 Infrequent buyers

Customer & Contact	Last Year's Business	This Year's Forecast

13

Table 1.4 Regular buying customers

Customer & Contact	Last Year's Business	This Year's Forecast	Excess/ Shortfall to date

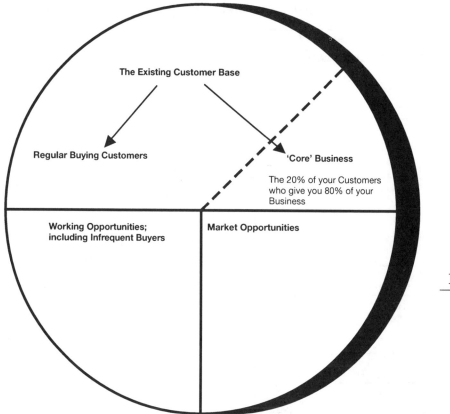

Fig. 1.3 Quantifying the existing customer base and the working opportunities

The first thing you will notice is that I have placed the infrequent buyers in the *working opportunities* area, the reasons for which will become clear when we consider the different strategies we will adopt with the different parts of the business MAP.

ANALYSING AND COMPLETING THE LIST

Now that we have a clear picture of where our customers are, we should begin to think about the prospects we are working on, i.e. the working opportunities.

Use Table 1.5 to compile your list of working opportunities.

15

Table 1.5 Working opportunities

Prospect & Contact	Nature & Size of Opportunity	Stage of Sale/ Probability %	Forecast

16

The third and fourth columns refer to the Stage of the Sale/ Probability percentage and Forecast respectively, but ignore these for the moment. We will return to them, later when their significance will become clearer.

Finally, using Table 1.6, compile your market opportunities list.

On this list I would like you to complete all four columns. If you can't, for any reason, you are probably deluding yourself that they have developed into market opportunities. They're probably only at the *research* stage.

Flow of the business MAP

17

Now that we have positively identified where the future business can be won, we need to look at the flow of the business MAP.

Your company's marketing effort, which would include *market research/information*, can identify your market opportunities. Once you have made contact, you will convert some of these to working opportunities and eventually you will convert some of these into customers, either infrequent buyers or regular buying customers.

There's more to be said later about both market and working opportunities, but if you look at Figure 1.4, you will begin to identify some potential problems within your existing customer base.

Table 1.6 Market opportunities

Prospect & 'Phone No.	Contact & Position	Nature of Opportunity	Size of Opportunity

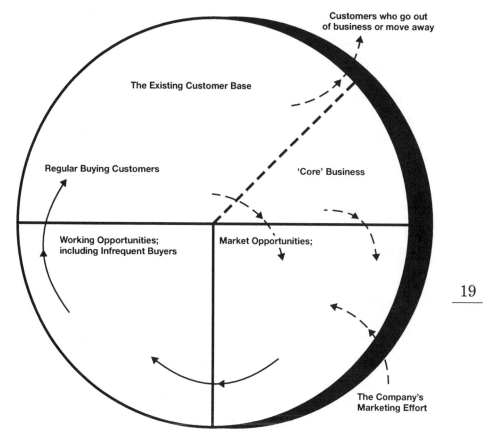

Fig. 1.4 The flow of the business map

19

Customer base problems

LOSING CUSTOMERS

You will see that you can lose customers through no fault of your own if they go out of business, or if they move away from your territory. There may also be situations where customers are taken over by other companies and the purchasing habits revert to those of the new owners. This can work for you as well as against you, i.e. your customers may take over companies with whom you have previously had little or no success. While there may be little or nothing you can do about losing customers in this way, you need to be constantly look-ing for indications that this may happen and always be building up a list of prospects as future replacements.

You should know your territory intimately, be studying the business press, and listening to views aired by other busi-nessmen about some of the companies with whom you deal. You don't need to become alarmist, but you do have to have your finger on the pulse, or these untoward happenings will take you by surprise. You know that in different economic cli-mates different types of business are at risk. If you're dealing with those types of businesses, you have to be on your guard.

The other way that you can lose business is by your cus-tomers becoming your competitors' market opportunities.

Later, we will look at ways of *building customer loyalty*, but in the meantime, look through your sales records for the past couple of years and calculate how many customers and how much business has been lost over that period – either because your customers went out of business/moved away, or because you lost them to the competition.

The remarkable thing that I often find, when I conduct this exercise in training courses, is that there is usually a fairly consistent figure in percentage terms of business over the years, which is why I now refer to the *annual dissipation rate* from your customer base.

Whatever this figure is, when you put together your action plan for achieving the new year's target, you will need to do so in the knowledge that there is a dissipation figure which will have to be replaced. If you find that it doesn't happen this year, or doesn't happen to the same extent as before, you are in a total winning position, because you will have already planned to replace that business and should therefore be well ahead of the game.

CUSTOMERS WHO GO OUT OF BUSINESS

Next, look at the customers who went out of business and try to identify a pattern. If there is one, you need to establish if it is simply that the business you are in is at risk in the current economy, or if there is something you are doing in the way that you are prospecting that is causing you to go for higher-risk customers.

I carried out some work with the motor trade a number of years ago and found that there was a distinct pattern to be observed where small companies were leasing vehicles on the terms that allowed them to make the smallest initial payment. That didn't pose a problem for the motor dealers, who were paid by the leasing companies, but it did present a major problem for the sales people who were negotiating the leasing.

Many leasing companies thereafter changed their policy with regard to the size of the initial payments, unless very strong documentary evidence was forthcoming regarding the soundness of the prospective lessee. This move, which I believe was entirely necessary, was not helped by the fact that the people selling the cars often took the line of least resistance in order to make the sale, and tried very hard to keep the initial payments down to the minimum, but it did eventually work.

LOSING CUSTOMERS TO COMPETITION

You may now want to try to identify a pattern of reasons why some of your existing customer base becomes someone else's

21

market opportunities. *Is it a company problem or a management problem or is it YOU?*

If there is a pattern and you have identified the problem, you need to do something about it very quickly, because common sense tells you that it must be easier to do business with people you already know than to constantly have to find new customers. If the problem is *you*, talk to your manager or your colleagues, but get it sorted out before you become demotivated. The job of selling can be tough enough when you want to do it: it becomes absolutely impossible when you don't. If it is genuinely *a company or management problem* and your company won't do anything to rectify the problem, LEAVE! Join a company who either doesn't have the problem or is prepared to address problems like these when and if they arise.

22

At the end of the day, what we are trying to identify is the amount of business on an annual basis that we have to replace, and that's before we take into consideration any increase in targets over last year.

Let's now go back and look at your core business.

How many customers make up your core business?

The more you have the safer you are, because if one of these should be lost to you, you need the impact to be as small as possible. If you have one customer who gives you 80 per cent of your business, you're not selling anything to them, they are buying from you and are therefore in the driving seat. They will wield as much power as they can muster to dictate; terms, prices, delivery schedules, product specifications, the lot!

Let us now look at your regular buying customers.

Within the group who represent your regular buying customers, what percentage of their available business are you getting? And, what can you do to increase this, so as to move them over towards the core business part of your MAP?

Finally, consider some of the activities both you and the rest of your company can carry out to prevent your customer base becoming the competitors' market opportunities:

- 'Locking in' activities like annual contracts, service contracts, warranty conditions, etc.

- Offering 'added value' in your service to the customer.

We will look at these again in more detail when we discuss building customer loyalty, for now we will move on to the next chapter and look at *quality of activity*.

SUMMARY

- *You cannot get the business if you don't know where it is!*

- The business can only come from your *existing customer base,* your *working opportunities* and your *market opportunities.*

- Break your *existing customer base* into *core business* and *regular buying customers.*

- Identify your *infrequent buyers* and regard them as only *working opportunities.*

- Recognise that you will have an *annual dissipation rate* from your *existing customer base.* Find out the *reasons* why this happens – and do something about it.

- Know that you will need to change to meet the demands of an ever changing market place and that if you don't, your company will be more than likely to change you!

2

Quality of activity

'What gets measured gets done'
TOM PETERS

In the early 1990s, Tom Peters, undoubtedly *the* business guru of the 80s and 90s, conducted a seminar in London called 'The Customer Revolution Conference', based on his book, Thriving On Chaos. This seminar was filmed by BBC Education and Training and sold for training purposes under the title, 'The Tom Peters Experience'.

In one part of his seminar he talks about *measuring the quality of customer service* and I have always been convinced that this thinking can also be applied to the **quality of activity**. The next section in this book is primarily concerned with *identifying* and *measuring* the quality of activity.

Let us look at the Market Opportunities in your Business MAP. *What is the conversion ratio between your market opportunities and your working opportunities?*

In short, for every ten prospects that you contact with a view to setting up a meaningful call, with how many do you succeed? Now try to identify the reasons for the failure of some of these. This is usually the first step in identifying a *training need*, the most common of which in this part of your business MAP is **appointment making skills**. The simple fact of life is that you can't sell to prospects if you don't get in front of them. Of course there may be other reasons, such as:

- The prospect has no genuine need for your product or service.
- You are speaking to the wrong person.

Both of these suggest to me that the failure is at the market information stage and these shouldn't even be regarded as market prospects.

Now let us look at the Working Opportunities in your Business MAP, and conduct the same exercise. *What is the conversion ratio from working opportunities to buying customers, including first time, infrequent and regular buyers.*

25

Now I would like you to identify the different stages of the sale in your business, for example,

- fact finding or information gathering calls
- site or factory visits
- trials
- testing of samples
- presentations to individuals or groups, etc.

Depending on your business, there will be some of these and more.

When you have done this, I would like you to identify at what stage in the sale you lose most opportunities. This will identify other training needs.

In the early stages these could include:

- Failing to identify a need or desire for your product or service – poor questioning and information gathering skills.

- Failure only at the time of *asking for the order*, could either mean poor product presentation skills or poor closing technique.

- Failure at either the *trial* or *sample stages* would suggest, if your product is on a par with your competition, that you may have *oversold* the product and built the prospect's expectations too high. This would most commonly indicate poor product knowledge rather than simply over-enthusiasm.

Many sales people with whom I have worked over the years, fail to recognise that prospects and customers are usually busy people. It's one of the reasons that we make appointments, to be sure of getting to see them at a time which is mutually convenient. That being the case, why should they see you at all, if there is no genuine desire on their part to know about the product or service that you're offering?

People only see you when there is something you have which they think they might want. Therefore failure in the working opportunities part of your MAP, suggests that in the majority of situations, there is something that you have done which is not of the quality that it should have been.

> Remember that prospects and customers don't **fail to buy,** sales people **fail to sell!**

Before I move on from this section, I know that some of you reading this book will assert that the main reason for your failure to sell is **price!**

That may be a reason in some circumstances, but should definitely not be the case in the majority. The fact that your company is viable in the area of price with your existing customers means that you don't always lose out on price.

If price *is* the genuine reason, it either indicates:

- your company's pricing policy may be out of touch with the market, or

- your ability to handle price objections and early price challenges is poor (another training need).

It is probably now appropriate to revisit the diagram of your business MAP to see how it is developing. See Figure 2.1.

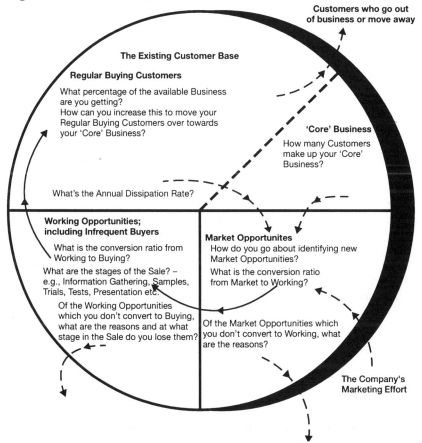

Fig. 2.1 Measuring effectiveness and what's in the 'pipeline'

While the diagram is obviously fairly busy looking, it does help your understanding of the concept to be able to see it all on one page.

You will also notice that I have included two very important questions in the diagram within the group who represent your regular buying customers:

1 What percentage of the available business are you getting?
2 What can you do to increase this so as to move them over towards the Core Business part of your MAP?

The following exercise will underline the importance of these questions.

Backward planning to ensure future results

I would now like to take you through a small exercise in backward planning to show you how mapping the business will help you ensure your future results.

For the purposes of this exercise, let us assume that your ability to convert market opportunities into working opportunities is one in four, i.e. for every four prospects whom you contact you secure qualified appointments with one of them. For some of you this may seem a very low figure, but for others it will appear to be outrageously high.

Similarly, let us assume that the conversion from working opportunities to buying customers is one in three. Again I would point out that these are purely arbitrary figures to demonstrate the example.

In the existing customer base, you have an annual dissipation rate of 5 per cent, and your target, in financial terms, for the new year is a 10 per cent increase on your previous year's performance of £100,000 and is therefore £110,000. Note that one of the reasons for the 10 per cent uplift in your target is the expectation by your company that there will be organic growth within your existing customer base of 5 per cent.

If we deduct the 5 per cent dissipation figure and make allowances for the 5 per cent organic growth, we are left with £99,750 which we forecast will come from the existing customer base. Of this figure, 80 per cent or £79,800 will come from *core business*, with the balance of £19,950 coming from the *regular buyers*.

The first thing we have to do is calculate the average financial turnover of business that we can expect from each of the regular buying customers, and again for the purposes of the exercise, let us put this at £200 per customer. This means that there are 100 customers among our regular buyers, which by applying the '80/20' rule tells us that we have approximately 25 customers making up our *core business* (when you conduct this calculation in real life, later in this chapter, remember to exclude your infrequent buyers as this will drive your average down to an inaccurate level).

The shortfall between our forecast and our target is £10,250 and can only come to us via the working and market opportunities. Using our conversion ratios, we now know that during the course of the year we need to be working on £30,750 of potential business, calling on 154 prospects. I have applied the average for the *regular buying customers* here as it is unusual for working opportunities to go straight to core business, except in the case of national, major and key accounts.

If we now apply the conversion ratio from market to working, we know that in order to achieve the target, we need to identify £123,000 of opportunities. Figure 2.2 helps make the situation clearer.

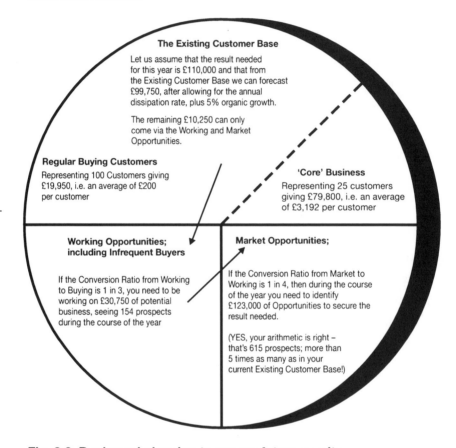

The Existing Customer Base

Let us assume that the result needed for this year is £110,000 and that from the Existing Customer Base we can forecast £99,750, after allowing for the annual dissipation rate, plus 5% organic growth.

The remaining £10,250 can only come via the Working and Market Opportunities.

Regular Buying Customers

Representing 100 Customers giving £19,950, i.e. an average of £200 per customer

'Core' Business

Representing 25 customers giving £79,800, i.e. an average of £3,192 per customer

Working Opportunities; including Infrequent Buyers

If the Conversion Ratio from Working to Buying is 1 in 3, you need to be working on £30,750 of potential business, seeing 154 prospects during the course of the year

Market Opportunities;

If the Conversion Ratio from Market to Working is 1 in 4, then during the course of the year you need to identify £123,000 of Opportunities to secure the result needed.

(YES, your arithmetic is right – that's 615 prospects; more than 5 times as many as in your current Existing Customer Base!)

Fig. 2.2 Backward planning to ensure future results

I would guess that your initial reaction would be that these figures can't be achieved and you may be right. In training room situations when I carry out this exercise, the reaction of many sales people is that the target is obviously too high.

I don't agree. A 10 per cent uplift on sales where organic

growth of 5 per cent can reasonably be expected doesn't seem unattainable to me. Were some of you to apply the figures in this exercise to your own situation, you would probably find that there are simply not enough market opportunities to make it happen.

Good! That forces us to address the real issues, which are the **Conversion Ratios**. You will only be able to deliver the target if you improve the conversion ratios. I have worked with many companies who faced the problem highlighted in this exercise, in their real-life situations, so I know that what follows can and does work.

With good *product training* and good *sales technique training*, you can usually expect to reduce the annual dissipation rate to 4 per cent; the saving coming from those customers you would otherwise lose to the competition – not from those who go out of business or move away. You can also increase your organic growth within your existing customer base to 7.5 per cent. The achievement of this will also be made easier for you if your company becomes involved in innovative marketing or product development and improvement.

When we have identified at what stages in the sale we lose most working opportunities, and address the problem, invariably by some form of training and retraining, it is reasonable to expect an improvement in this area from one in three to two in five. In the market opportunities area of our business MAP, with good appointment making skills, we can expect to improve this ratio from one in four to three in eight.

I hope that you have noticed that in every area I have sought to make small changes, not dramatic ones.

> *Small changes in behaviour can, and will, produce big results.*

Study the diagram which follows – Figure 2.3 – to see the impact of these small changes.

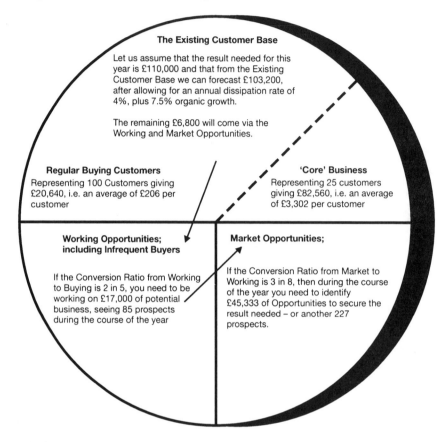

The Existing Customer Base

Let us assume that the result needed for this year is £110,000 and that from the Existing Customer Base we can forecast £103,200, after allowing for an annual dissipation rate of 4%, plus 7.5% organic growth.

The remaining £6,800 will come via the Working and Market Opportunities.

Regular Buying Customers
Representing 100 Customers giving £20,640, i.e. an average of £206 per customer

'Core' Business
Representing 25 customers giving £82,560, i.e. an average of £3,302 per customer

Working Opportunities; including Infrequent Buyers

If the Conversion Ratio from Working to Buying is 2 in 5, you need to be working on £17,000 of potential business, seeing 85 prospects during the course of the year

Market Opportunities;

If the Conversion Ratio from Market to Working is 3 in 8, then during the course of the year you need to identify £45,333 of Opportunities to secure the result needed – or another 227 prospects.

Fig. 2.3 Backward planning to ensure future results

If the target was unachievable before, it certainly isn't now.

It's now time to apply all of this thinking to your own situation, so that we can make sure that you achieve your sales targets.

You will need the following information:

- Your annual target.
- The dissipation rate from your existing customer base.

- The organic growth that you can reasonably expect from your existing customer base.

- The annual average produced from your regular buying customers.

- Your conversion ratio from working to buying.

- Your conversion ratio from market to working.

It may be that you haven't yet measured what the conversion ratios are, but I'm sure you can initially make an educated guess. Now put all of this information on the following diagram – Figure 2.4 – and work out the figures for your real-life situation in the same way as we did in the exercise.

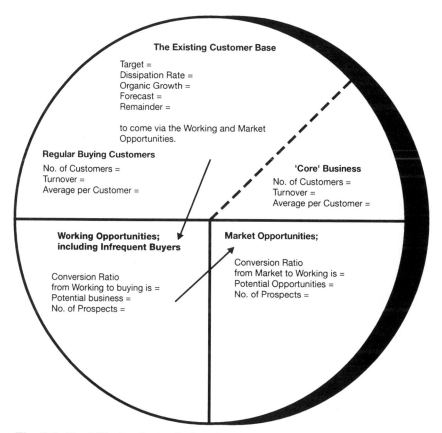

The Existing Customer Base

Target =
Dissipation Rate =
Organic Growth =
Forecast =
Remainder =

to come via the Working and Market Opportunities.

Regular Buying Customers

No. of Customers =
Turnover =
Average per Customer =

'Core' Business

No. of Customers =
Turnover =
Average per Customer =

Working Opportunities; including Infrequent Buyers

Conversion Ratio
from Working to buying is =
Potential business =
No. of Prospects =

Market Opportunities;

Conversion Ratio
from Market to Working is =
Potential Opportunities =
No. of Prospects =

Fig. 2.4 Real-life backward planning

Earlier in the book, I told you about working with a group of Direct Insurance sales people. During this type of exercise I asked them to tell me what their conversion ratios were. Their sales manager, with whom I enjoyed tremendous rapport, said that he reckoned the average conversion from working to buying was one in four. My reply to that was, *Don't be silly, it can't be that bad.*

He left for a while before returning with the actual figures, which averaged out at one in six.

Remember my belief that prospects don't agree to see sales people just for the hell of it. This fact is even more true of the Domestic Life Insurance business, therefore the only comment left to me was, *Don't ask yourself how good is one in six, ask yourself, who is getting the other five!*

When we came to their conversion from market to working, we discovered that it was one in ten, but what else would you expect from a group who thought that the local Telephone Directory was a list of market opportunities?

In the course of running their training programme we were able to put in place some better quality market research which produced *genuine* market opportunities. This resulted in improving the conversion ratio of one in ten to one in four, from this source alone. Thereafter, we instituted a programme of *referrals* and *preferrals*, about which there is more later in the book, and from this source we were able to achieve a conversion ratio of four in five.

The selling skills training, which is the subject of my book, *The Ultimate USP*, which is also published by Pitman Publishing, in the same series as this book, enabled us to achieve a conversion ratio from working to buying of two in three.

With results as impressive as these, which have been replicated in many companies in different industries, I am constantly vexed by organisations who don't place great emphasis on training, because they think it is expensive. If they think *training is expensive*, perhaps they should reconsider the real *cost of ignorance!*

At the beginning of this chapter, I referred to 'The Customer Revolution Conference' seminar conducted by Tom Peters in London, based on his book, *Thriving On Chaos*.

Here's another of his thoughts from that seminar;

'The Quality issue is a Training issue, and the level of Training in this country (the UK) and my country (the USA), if we have a radical improvement in the next five years it will then perhaps, if we're lucky, be up to merely disgusting.' . . .

'Train, Train, Train, Train and as soon as you're finished, re-Train, re-Train, re-Train. There's no issue as to whether everybody ought to be re-Trained all the time, and yet we behave as if there were'

Sadly, that has also been my experience.

The likelihood is that you are reading this book because *you chose* to do so. That being the case, it appears that you have taken your training issue into your own hands and that's encouraging. If your sales manager gave you this book, that's even more encouraging. When we look at *career development* and *personal development plans* later in this book we will explore further just how much you can try to get your company to do and how much you're going to have to do for yourself.

Measuring the effectiveness of activity

THE PROBABILITY OF SUCCESS

The crucial point in measuring the business that you have 'in the pipeline' is in the *existing customer base* and in the *working opportunities* parts of your business MAP. In both of these areas, you need to establish criteria for measuring the *probability of success*.

I have reprinted below an example of one of these which came about when working with A & W Fullarton, the packaging company, which is part of the Macfarlane Group in Scotland (for those of you to whom that name doesn't mean a lot, the Macfarlane Group (Clansman) PLC is the highly successful £100 million turnover business headed up by Lord Macfarlane of Bearsden. He is one of Britain's few remaining 'captains of industry and commerce' who, at the time of writing, is also Chairman of United Distillers, part of Guinness PLC).

Success criteria

100 per cent probability

When you physically have the customer's order.

(There is a school of thought that believes that an order is only an order when the customer's money is in your company's bank account. As someone who runs his own business, I tend to agree!)

90 per cent probability

When the customer has agreed to buy from you and you are waiting for them to process their paperwork.

80 per cent probability

When you're told by the customer that they intend to order, pending the approval of a *'decision maker'*, and/or the run down of existing stocks.

70 per cent probability

When the customer tells you that they are going to place an order when they have received confirmation by your company of modified terms. (e.g. discounts, credit terms, etc.).

60 per cent probability

When you have established that the customer needs your product or service, can afford it and is going to order from *you* . . . but can't commit to when that will be.

37

50 per cent probability

When you have established that the customer wants your product or service and has the money, and the decision is between you and one other competitor.

If you can't fit the situation into one of the above, the likelihood of success is too low to be measured **yet**.

It may be that you will have to modify these to suit your own business, but a measurement of this type is extremely important, because in the next chapter we will be looking at the *strategic considerations* to be taken into account when determining your next activity on the basis of the current probability.

Refer back to Chapter 1 and the table we produced for examining your *working opportunities* and complete the third and fourth columns, for each individual opportunity, as shown in the following example:

WORKING OPPORTUNITIES

Prospect & Contact	Nature & Size of Opportunity	Stage of Sale/ Probability %	Forecast
A	£1000	80%	£800
B	£5000	Info. gathering	not yet
C	£6000	70%	£4,200
D	£2000	90%	£1,800
Total	£14,000		£6,800

You will need to create a similar table for *progressing the existing customer base,* as follows:

PROGRESSING THE EXISTING CUSTOMER BASE

Customer & Contact	Nature & Size of Opportunity	Stage of Sale/ Probability %	Forecast

By multiplying the opportunity size by the probability figure, you will arrive at your first stab at realistic forecasting. You will also notice that there is one situation in the working opportunities example where the stage of the sale can be 'logged', but it is too early yet to allocate a probability figure, therefore there is no forecast figure which can be applied until such time as you can allocate that *probability of success.*

However, what follows is an interesting discovery I made a number of years ago when working with a major client in the

UK. They applied this concept, *exactly*, and when they re-examined the accuracy of their forecasting, they discovered that a 'you win some – you lose some' type of principle had taken effect, with the result that consistently over a period of two to three years, the difference between their forecast and what had been the final result, was never more than 10 per cent.

Another very important fact emerged. Once any selling situation has reached the stage where a probability of success can be put against it, any *meaningful selling call* made on that opportunity means that the percentage figure can only go up or down – it cannot remain the same!

39

This could represent some really bad news for some of the sales people with whom I have met and worked. Because I don't know of a single sales person, myself included, who has not occasionally 'padded' his or her call report! If you are **the one**, please accept my apologies and congratulations, but permit me my scepticism.

- Have you never overslept and called into a nearby customer for a quick coffee and a chat with the receptionist, secretary or even the customer (if you know him or her that well) so that you could put it in your Call Report?

- Have you never had the situation when an appointment was cancelled at short notice, therefore you called in 'on spec.' to another customer so that you could make up your quota of daily calls?

- Have you never had the situation where you quite simply didn't make any call at all, but you knew that it wouldn't be checked so you indulged in a little creativity to make yourself look busy?

- Ever taken time off for a sneaky game of golf, or some very important shopping?

- Perhaps called in to see an 'old friend' because you happened to be in the area, or taken a customer for lunch which lasted much longer than you anticipated?

Well, before you rise up in righteous indignation, let me tell you. I have done all of these and more, which was one of the few things that my sales teams used to hate about me! They couldn't pull a stroke I hadn't used or hadn't seen being used.

The only thing that I have seen in my years in sales and management that is more creative than sales people's call reports is their expenses claims.

However, all of these, for any sensible sales manager, are the characteristics that also make their staff effective and creative when they are actually doing the job. That's why, as a manager, I never had a problem with it, as long as it was controlled. The key message is that whenever you make a *meaningful* selling call, you can only improve or impair the probability of success.

Perhaps we should now consider some of the questions you should be asking yourself, when you try to evaluate how successful you will be with either the working opportunities or with all or any of your existing customer base whenever you are trying to sell to them.

These include:

- Does the customer have the money? If not, can you offer the means to get the money?

- What are the customer's previous buying habits?

- Has the customer previously dealt successfully with either you or your company?
- Is this going to be a major decision for the customer?
- What about internal conflicts – e.g. does someone in the company, who can influence the decision, have an otherwise 'vested interest'?
- What about the customer's priorities – e.g. is there another financial demand conflicting with what you're trying to sell?
- Is the customer prepared to make some type of formal commitment – e.g. a letter of intent, a purchase order number or written confirmation of a verbal agreement?
- Will the decision be influenced by timing or seasonal trends?
- Who else is competing for this business?
- How high is your contact level within the decision-making process?
- Will the decision be affected by outside market forces – e.g. interest rates, government action, the weather, etc?
- How well have you identified the customer's needs – i.e. why should he or she buy from *you*?
- How good is the quality of your proposal and your presentation?
- Is the customer a member of an influencing or buying group?
- Will it be all or nothing – i.e. could you get *some* of the business if you don't get it all?

THE SIGNIFICANCE OF MAPPING THE BUSINESS

Mapping the Business allows you to take into consideration the typical 'lead time' in your business. That is, the time delay between when you begin your discussions with your prospects and customers and when the order is placed. If there is no real lead time in your business, then you literally take each day as it comes. If the lead time is one week, then this week's orders will come from last week's activity.

Take the example of my own business where the typical lead time is five months. This means that when my financial year ends at the end of December, my results for the year are dictated, on the whole, by my activity up to the end of July. There are always exceptions of course, and I can occasionally secure some extra business at a few weeks' notice but the converse is that I have some clients who have taken more than a year to make up their minds.

I had a client whose lead time was 18 months and another where it was four years! This effectively meant, for the latter of these, that at the end of 1993 the result expected for the years '94, '95 and '96 had already been determined.

MORTGAGING YOUR FUTURE

What should happen is that, allowing for your own lead time, the results will more or less follow a distinct pattern relating to your previous activity. However, what happens when there has been a reduction in either the quantity or quality of that activity?

Initially, nothing!

The results will still be coming through from your previous activity. Your lack of activity will probably not be noticed, because these results are still coming in. Then, in line with the lead time, there will be a fall off in your results. This is when your sales manager calls you into the office and has a chat about the poor results.

What usually happens at this stage is that you go along to some of your best customers and talk them into bringing forward some of the business which you have in the pipeline and your sales manager thinks that the little 'pep' talk has had an effect and that everything is back to normal.

Well, it isn't.

You have simply *mortgaged your future results* and postponed the bad news till a slightly later date. You may be able to increase and improve your activity so that you eventually recover from the situation, but what is more likely is that a 'domino effect' will come into play and adversely affect your original activity plan, the purpose of which was to secure the results expected of you in future weeks and months.

This is not the type of position in which you would want to find yourself, but it happens. Quite often, however, this situation will become out of hand and at this time, many sales people will decide to leave the company and look for another job. Interestingly, at the time of resigning, there will be no mention of lack of activity, but lots of excuses will be put forward for the lack of results in an attempt, usually subconsciously, to shift the blame for the poor performance.

This situation is very sad when it is self inflicted, but even worse when the sales management team, in their ignorance, create the problem for you. How many times has your manager asked you to pull forward some business in order to get it in before the end of the financial year?

How many times has there been a bad month in a sales team due to the poor performance of other individuals and you have been asked by your manager to pull forward some business to make up someone else's deficit on behalf of the

43

team? All that's happened is that your manager has mort-gaged *your* future, and his or hers and the company's.

If this has never happened to you, you are one of the lucky ones, but trust me, if you stay in selling long enough it will happen to you! If you can, resist it – or get your manager to give me a call. However, don't become despondent, we will look at **Activity Plans** in the next chapter which will help you prevent and overcome this type of situation.

In the late 1980s, I was conducting this exercise with the specialist adviser team of one of Europe's largest merchant banks and I knew that in the room was one particular advis-er who was currently going through a bad time, but had pre-viously been a star performer. His performance-related earnings had been two to three times that of his nearest con-temporary and was of the order of 20 times the national aver-age earnings in his native country, but he was, at the time of my presentation, on an all time low. At the end of my session when I was taking questions and comments he stood before his colleagues and stated quite categorically, 'That's the first time that anybody has been able to show me what I'm doing wrong'. After our training session finished, I agreed to meet with him again for a couple of in-depth sessions on mapping his business, and I'm pleased to be able to say that, consis-tently over the five years that have elapsed since then, his performance and his earnings have been restored to their former glory.

SOME BENEFITS OF 'MAPPING THE BUSINESS'

I have listed below, some of the benefits of what we have gone through so far:

- You will always be ahead by measuring what's in your pipeline.

- You will be able to take quick action to ensure the results.

- You will be able to make better use of the resources available to you.

- You will create a real link between your efforts and your results.

- You will be able to produce better and more realistic forecasts.

- You will be able to minimise 'seat of the pants' type operating.

- You will create a better balance between long and short term results.

- You will identify your training and development needs earlier.

- You will improve your own motivation by measuring your efforts as well as your results.

- You will improve your self-discipline, because you know that you can hide behind results, but you can't hide behind the measurement of your activity.

- You can never guarantee your results, but you can always guarantee your activity.

In closing this chapter, I would refer you back to the first diagram that we used in chapter 1: *'Securing the sales results'*.

- **Step 1** of that diagram has had to be assumed, whether it happened or not.

- **Step 2** will have been imposed 'from above', whether you liked it or not.

- **Step 4** will also have been imposed, and with any luck you

45

may even have been able to make some meaningful input into it.

- **Step 3**, although it should have come before **Step 4**, we have now conducted on your own previous results.

Perhaps this has not been in the depth that I would achieve in a face-to-face situation, but at least we now have a good idea of how this year's target relates to last year's results.

In the next chapter we will look at **Steps 5** and **6** and by the time that we've reached the end of the book, we will have covered the whole process.

SUMMARY

- As well as *monitoring the quantity* of your activity, you need to *measure the quality* of it.

- Make sure that you know what your *conversion ratios* are in the various parts of your Business **MAP**.

- Conduct regular *backward planning exercises* – so that you know exactly what you need to do to bring in the results.

- Put in place a system to enable you to measure the *probability of success* with your working opportunities and your existing customers.

- Don't *mortgage your future* to provide a short-term solution – and don't let anyone else do it to you either!

3

Identifying the direction of activity

'Efficiency is doing things properly;
*Effectiveness is doing the **proper** things!'*

I used that expression in the Introduction to this book, and this is where it applies. *Direction of activity* is all about *doing the proper things.*

Look back to the working opportunities part of your business MAP and try to identify the average number of calls it takes to get an order or indeed a negative decision. As we go through this chapter you will begin to identify that there is also a time when you should walk away from a situation and take your activity in a more meaningful *direction*.

Hopefully, based on your own input, it will also become clear to you when that is, in your business. Now go through your existing customer base, including core business, and calculate the frequency and therefore the number of calls you have to make on those.

Use the following diagram – Figure 3.1 – to help you build up the picture.

You will notice that I haven't yet made any reference to the market opportunities. That will come shortly. Now you need to calculate the number of selling days that you have in a year, normally around the **200** mark.

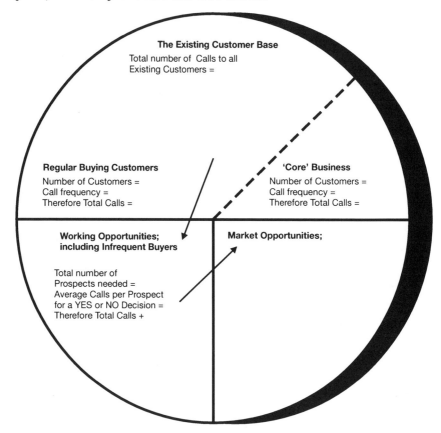

Fig. 3.1 Creating a meaningful action plan

In case you doubt this figure, calculate the following:

1 In 52 weeks, there are **260** selling days. Most sales people have around four or five weeks of vacation, i.e. 20 to 25 days. I'll stick with 20 for the moment. That leaves **240** selling days.

2 In most countries there are around nine Statutory or Bank Holidays. That leaves **231** selling days.

3 For most of you, there will be at least one full day sales

meeting per month, i.e. 12 days. That leaves **219** selling days.

4 There will always be a few days of sickness, the occasional family happening such as funerals and weddings etc. If my experiences are typical, that should come to about another five days. That leaves us with **214** selling days.

5 The days needed for administration and paperwork etc., will easily come to 14, which is why I use the figure of **200 selling days**.

You may have noticed that I made no allowance for training days, although I hope for some of you that this also needs to be deducted. Neither have I made any allowance for 'telephone days', mainly because it doesn't apply in all businesses, and when I cover the subject of the *mobile office*, you will find that there are alternatives to 'telephone days'.

When I run this exercise in a training room environment it is invariably easier than I find it here in this book, because I can get immediate feedback about the average number of calls in a day. However, in the majority of the businesses with which I have been involved, I worked on around seven selling calls per day, with three or four of those having been set up as fixed appointments.

I do recall, however, conducting a sales training course with a group of people some of whom worked with Coats Patons, the thread manufacturer, where the figure was 'slightly' different. The people with whom I was working were with the retail sales force who sold to shops etc. I asked the question about the number of calls per day to be told by one member of the team that it was 16 calls per day. The expression on my face was enough to convey my surprise, when the same person continued, 'It would be 17, but somebody keeps stopping me to ask what I'm selling'.

Although I asked you to put together the number of calls per year from your business MAP, in practice you need to be flexible, so I would like you only to consider the next three months. Create a table similar to that shown below – Table 3.1 – and fill in the information for your next three months targets and activity plans.

You will see that I have made room in this example to allow you to break your target down by products. It may be that your target is not produced this way, in which case simply put the total. I have then gone on to break your activity plan down into the various areas of your business MAP, in line with the exercise that we have recently completed. You will also note that in this table I have included market opportunities, which we didn't previously address.

Some of you will set up your appointments by 'cold calling' and some by telephone. If they are all cold calls you will be able to put an exact figure in here and ignore the reference to telephone calls. If, however, they are all by telephone or a mix of telephone and cold calls, you will need to consider how many telephone calls you have to make to set up an appointment.

All of the clients with whom I have worked in recent years agree that the average figure to set up an appointment is five telephone calls, for some of the following reasons:

- The customer or prospect may not be available.
- You may have difficulty in getting past the receptionist or secretary.
- You will occasionally find you have the wrong person.

Table 3.1 Three month target and activity plans

TARGETS FOR THE PERIOD	From:	To:	(3 months)
Financial Targets:	Target		
Product 'A'	£		
Product 'B'	£		
Product 'C'	£		
Total	£		
Activity Targets:			
Calls per Selling Day:			
No. of Selling Days:			
Total Calls:			
The Business MAP	No. of Customers	Calls per Customer	Total Calls
Core Business			
Regular Buying Customers			
	No. of Opportunities	Calls per Opportunities	Total Calls
Working Opportunities			
Marketing Opportunities;			
Cold Calls			
Telephone Calls			Total Calls =

If you go back to the exercise we carried out in chapter 2 when we determined the conversion ratios and the working and market opportunities needed, you will see I have transferred these figures in the following example to clarify your understanding. The figures used are where the conversion ratios have been improved and I have also worked on the following assumptions, which are based on the way I operated when I was full time 'In the field':

In the period which I have taken there are **64** selling days. I have deducted:

1 Two Public Holidays for the New Year period, although in Scotland that is usually considerably more.
2 Three days for sales meetings.
3 Six days (i.e. 12 half days), for telephone appointment making. I only ever worked by telephone appointment, having tried cold calling and found that, for me, it wasn't as successful.
4 One day for family happenings as mentioned before.
5 I also deducted six days, i.e. two days per month, for essential administration and paperwork when I had to be in my office to be able to complete it.
6 Finally, two days for training in this period.

On the subject of essential paperwork, I don't consider filling in my expenses to be essential paperwork. I always do this in my own time at home.

If I worked for a progressive organisation I would expect them to allocate a minimum of 4 per cent of my time for training which took me off the road, i.e. eight days per year, hence the figure for the period. I aim for seven calls per day, four of which are by appointment, and I visit my core business once per month.

I have classified my regular buying customers such that the call pattern is as follows:

- 20 per cent of them are called on once per month.
- 30 per cent of them are called on once every six weeks.
- 50 per cent of them are called on once every three months.

My average number of calls to secure business from a working opportunity is two. (I will be looking at how to classify customers later in this chapter.) Therefore my table looks like Table 3.2 (overleaf).

Some of you may have noticed that there is a discrepancy between the number of calls that I can make within the selling days and the actual number I have planned. This has nothing to do with any of the call report 'padding' I referred to earlier, it is to make allowance for 'Murphy's' or 'Sod's' Law (one and the same thing), which states, **'If something can go wrong, it will!'** The longer you're in selling the more you will realise that this is true.

I have built into my activity plan an allowance to handle emergency situations so that these shouldn't disrupt my plan. The analogy would be:

If you're constantly driving your car at 100 per cent of its capability, what do you have in reserve if something goes wrong?

Nothing!

Well, what would make you think that working your territory is any different?

I will give you my money-back guarantee that if you drive yourself to 100 per cent of your capability in terms of time,

Table 3.2 Three month target and activity plans (a model)

TARGETS FOR THE PERIOD	From: January	To: March	(3 months)
Financial Targets:	Target		
Product 'A'	£15,000		
Product 'B'	£8,000		
Product 'C'	£4,500		
Total	£27,500		
Activity Targets:			
Calls per Selling Day:	7		
No. of Selling Days:	44		
Total Calls:	308		
The Business MAP	No. of Customers	Calls per Customer	Total Calls
Core Business	25	3	75
Regular Buying Customers	100	Average of 1.7	170
	No. of Opportunities	Calls per Opportunities	Total Calls
Working Opportunities	22	Average of 2	44
Marketing Opportunities;	57	5*	285*
Cold Calls	0		
Telephone Calls	*= 'Phone Calls		Total Calls = 289

you're heading for the 'funny farm' sooner rather than later. If your sales manager is reading this, make her or him look at the figures again. I am hardly recommending an easy life. The calls still represent almost 94 per cent of capability.

I have created a contingency plan of 19 calls in three months which represents three selling days, one per month. If disaster doesn't strike, you will have a splendid opportunity to use the extra time allowed to set up more market or working opportunities. Keeping ahead of the game is what it's all about.

Now that we have put together an overview of our targets and our activity plan for the next three months, we need to check that it's constantly on course, by creating '**stages**' for each of these. The following table – Table 3.3 – shows you how I have broken the targets into manageable stages. Now that you understand the concept, I have combined the table and the example from our earlier exercise.

Table 3.3 'Staged' financial targets (a model)

RESULTS – 'STAGED'	January	February	March
Financial Targets:			
Product 'A' – Target/Achieved	£4,800/£	£5,100/£	£5,100/£
Product 'B' – Target/Achieved	£2,600/£	£2,700/£	£2,700/£
Product 'C' – Target/Achieved	£1,500/£	£1,500/£	£1,500/£
Total Target/Achieved	£8,900/£	£9,300/£	£9,300/£

One of the many advantages of creating this type of staging is the ability to modify your plans in the light of things going wrong. What would you do if your achievement against target for the first month falls short by 10 per cent?

Most of the sales people that I have observed would do one of the following:

1 Try to recover the shortfall in the next month.
2 Put that month down to a bad experience and hope to make it up with an over-achievement later in the year.
3 Utter the infamous expression, 'Don't worry boss, it will be all right by the end of the year'.

My experience is that it is seldom 'all right by the end of the year'.

My recommendation would be to take the shortfall and spread it over the next two months. In this way you've adjusted the target so that it's more likely to be achieved and you're still keeping track of the cumulative figure you need to deliver.

In Table 3.4, I've carried out the same exercise on the activity plan.

As well as creating stages for the *quantity* of activity, you will see that I have included the ability to measure the *quality* factors. This is crucial, as this measurement is the advance warning that you're doing something wrong in one of these areas and in these circumstances would make you look at the possibility of a training need.

In relation to your telephone to appointment ratio, if you have difficulty measuring this, Table 3.5 may help.

Use a simple tick system for each time you physically dial a number (not wrong numbers) and tick each time you gain an appointment. Whenever you have been unsuccessful with the secretary or receptionist, make a tick. Similarly when you manage to get through to the prospect or customer, tick when you've been unsuccessful.

Finally, make a note of the various objections you encounter when trying to make the appointment, particularly those which you were unable to overcome. We will revisit these in the section on telephone appointment making.

Table 3.4 'Staged' activity plan (a model)

QUANTITY OF ACTIVITY – 'STAGED'	January	February	March
Selling Days – Target/Actual	14/	15/	15/
Core Business – Target/Actual	25/	25/	25/
Regular Buying – Target/Actual	54/	58/	58/
Working Opportunities – Target/Actual	14/	15/	15/
Market Opportunities – Target/Actual	19/	19/	19/
Cold Calls – Target/Actual	0/	0/	0/
Total Calls – Target/Actual	93/	98/	98/
Telephone Calls – Target/Actual	95/	95/	95/
QUALITY OF ACTIVITY Conversion Ratios			
Market to Working – Target/Actual	3 in 8/	3 in 8/	3in 8/
Working to Buying – Target/Actual	2 in 5/	2 in 5/	2 in 5/
Calls per Order – Target/Actual	2/	2/	2/
'Phone to Appointment – Target/Actual	5/	5/	5/

57

If you refer back to the original diagram in chapter 1 where we looked at how to *Secure the sales results*, you will be aware that we have completed **Steps 5** and **6**. Now what we need to do is ensure that we put our activity plan into action.

Table 3.5 Telephone strike rate: measuring the call to appointment ratio

'Phone Calls made	Appointments gained	Failure at Secretary or Receptionist	Failure at Prospect Customer	Objections encountered

Territory management: geographically

THE 'CLOVER LEAF' PRINCIPLE

The idea behind the 'clover leaf' principle is to get you out and working on your territory as quickly as possible, and keep you out there. Divide your territory into manageable areas, similar to *Figure 3.2*.

When you begin to divide up your territory, bear in mind the following:

■ Where your existing customers are located.

■ The geographic areas which offer the best opportunities for prospecting for 'new business'.

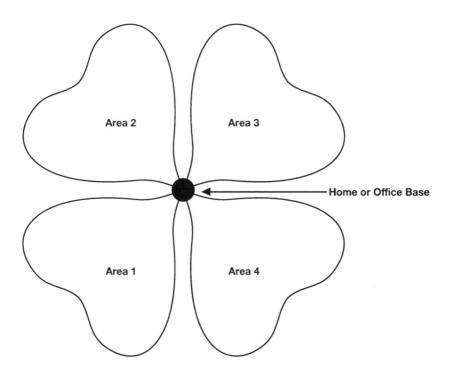

Fig. 3.2 The 'clover leaf' principle – division of territory

Each area should contain a roughly equal balance of customers and prospects.

In the diagram I have placed your base at the centre of your territory, whereas this may not be the case. You may have to adjust the base slightly to compensate. However, you should all be living on your territory, more or less, so the principle remains the same.

There may be some of you who work a very large territory and need to live away from home for periods of time. Simple! Live in an hotel or other accommodation at the centre of each area in which you intend to work, then break that area down into a clover leaf.

In my example I have broken the territory into four areas. If you can't do this, break it down into a number of areas which is not divisible by five, for reasons soon to become clear.

I recently carried out this exercise with a group of sales people, one of whom covered Eire. When I asked him to break his territory into a number of areas not divisible by five, he listed the 26 counties of that country! With that experience fresh in my mind, I will try to make my point a lot clearer in this book.

Keep the number of areas relatively small, certainly under ten. If you look at Figure 3.3 you will see how I have progressed this thinking whereby I have 'plotted' the appointment and non-appointment calls.

I am still working on my seven calls per day target, which we've already discussed; you may have to modify this to suit your business.

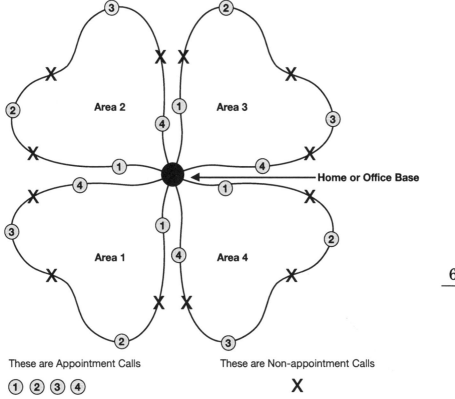

These are Appointment Calls ① ② ③ ④

These are Non-appointment Calls X

Fig .3.3 The 'clover leaf' principle – appointments and non-appointments

The first call in the morning should, where possible, be an appointment call. So should the last one in the afternoon. Whenever I had sales people who didn't have an early morning appointment which they had to attend, they invariably found something else 'important' to do before they started working their territories. *Like taking the children to school!*

Get yourself out in the morning and plan your territory so that you work in a 'loop' which throws you further away from your base until the afternoon when you can begin to work your way back. If you don't do this, the temptation to return home during the day may be irresistible.

I have plotted the territory such that there are four appointment calls in the day with a non-appointment call between each. This means that if one of the appointments falls down you will still be in an area where you can fill in with other non-appointment calls until the next appointment time.

When organising your areas, remember that each area should be worked in a sequence which allows for emergency calls to be made without too much disruption to your plan. You will also need to consider the following:

- The appointments you have made.

- That there will be certain non-appointment calls where there is definitely a 'right' time to make these.

- The length of time in each call.

- Other activities which can be undertaken between calls, e.g. cold call prospecting, telephoning for future appointments etc.

In the course of my work, it is standard practice for me to spend some time with the sales people working in the field before I design the training so that I can improve my understanding of the culture of the sale in their business. I also work with them afterwards so that I can see what progress has been made as a result of the training. I was recently involved in the latter of these exercises with a sales person from a pharmaceutical company when the following occurred, even after my training.

The sales person in question arranged to pick me up at my

hotel at 07.30, whereupon we drove about 70 miles due west to the first call. From there we travelled a further 100 miles due east to the next, came back very close to our starting-off point for the third, and headed about 40 miles due north for the fourth. As we chatted in the car on the return to my hotel base, this young man seemed to be very proud of the fact that he covered some 46,000 miles per year in his car.

Even if we don't take account of the cost of all of this travelling and the fact that his company car had to be replaced every 15 months or so, I did make the point that he was supposed to be a professional sales person, not a taxi driver!

63

THE ROLLING FIVE-WEEK PLAN

Now that you've planned the territory, you need to plan how you spend your days.

The *rolling five-week plan* in the way that I use it, is driven by appointments. If your business is not appointment driven, you will need to modify the system to plan your fixed call schedule instead. Look at Table 3.6.

I have produced a simple piece of paper here which controls everything that I do. I have selected four times in the day when I would make appointments. The first one is early and gets me out. The second and third keep me out and the fourth is on my way back to base. There is also enough time in between each to fit in a non-appointment call. There are some of you reading this book, who would only make four calls per day and if this is the case I would suggest that your business is such that these would all be appointment calls.

Table 3.6 Weekly call plan

Date/Day/Area	0830/0900	1100/1130	1330/1400	1600/1630
Date: Monday: Area:	Customer/Prospect Contact & Position Town & 'Phone No Call Objective Appt. Time			
Date: Tuesday: Area:				
Date: Wednesday: Area:				
Date: Thursday: Area:				
Date: Friday: Area:				

The times that I have used are for guideline purposes only, but begin early enough and finish late enough to ensure a full day. In addition, I have left enough time between, not only to fit in the other calls, but to give me time for a lengthy meeting, if required, without putting me under too much pressure to arrive at the next call on time.

In effect, this weekly call plan will take over from your diary. Thus, you will also see that I have included in the first box of this table, the information you need to note.

The first important thing about this type of call planning is that by breaking your territory into a number of areas which is not divisible by five, you have created a 'roll-over'.

65

For the sake of this exercise, let's assume that my territory is broken into four areas. This would mean that on the first day I would be in area one, on the second day in area two etc.

On the fifth day I am back in area one and on the first day of the following week I am back in area two.

I now have a situation whereby I will visit the same area on different days of the week, which will allow for some of the 'right times to call' situations to which I referred before. It also means that I know exactly when I will be back in that area, allowing me to arrange return appointments.

What I would like you to do is make up five sheets to cover the next five weeks. Start by blanking out any days when you can't work due to sales meetings, holidays, training etc. Now go through the pages filling in the remaining days, as follows:

1 If we assume that on day one you are in area one, and that days two and three are not available selling days, day four becomes area two etc.

2 Now fill in your fixed appointments for the next couple of weeks.

3 After that you may only be able to complete your rolling five-week plan in outline. However, at the end of every week you should be able to bring your plan up to date and outline another week.

This means that you constantly have a plan for the next five weeks ahead and are filling in fixed appointments as you arrange them. There is also another great advantage to using this type of plan, and that is when you are arranging appointments either by telephone or cold calling – with your plan in front of you, you can 'drive' the day and the time for appointments.

Appointments are supposed to be at mutual convenience so don't fall into the trap of having the customer drive the way that you plan your time. There will be occasions when this is unavoidable, but they will be far fewer than most sales people would have me believe.

I am continually being told that there is a customer with a large order who cannot wait and must be seen at a time which totally disrupts the rolling five-week plan. Nine times out of ten this is total rubbish! The fact is that the bigger the order, the more reasonable and professional the customer is likely to be. If you had an appointment with me for Tuesday at 11.00 o'clock and another customer insisted on meeting you at the same time, would you cancel my appointment?

If you ever did you would need to hope that I never found out – or your business relationship with me would come to a premature end. You need to arrange appointments which are convenient to both you and the customer. The five-week rolling plan makes this easier to do.

Territory management: strategically

CLASSIFYING CUSTOMERS

A great deal of your time will be spent with your existing customer base. It is therefore important that you make strategic decisions regarding how often you meet them, the purpose of the meetings, etc. I recommend that you classify your customers and to help you do this I have reproduced a classification format which has been used by one of my own clients. See Table 3.7.

Table 3.7 Customer classification

		A	B	C	D
	Penetration/ Potential Business	100% / 76%	75% / 51%	50% / 26%	25% / 0%
A	Over 100,000				
B	from 60 to 1000,000				
C	from 20 to 59,999				
D	from 15 to 19,999				
E	from 3 to 14,999				
F	from 1 to 2,999				
G	Up to 999				

Down the left-hand side of the table, the classification is by potential annual turnover and is broken down into seven groups, from A to G.

Along the top of the table is shown the amount of that business that you currently enjoy, broken into four groups, from A to D. This means that a customer who has been classified as D/C, has the ability to spend between £15,000 and £19,999 in the next year and you expect to win between 26 per cent and 50 per cent of that business.

In setting out your own classification system, you may want to change some of the figures. One of my clients prefers to classify the penetration figures as follows:

A = 56% and over
B = 21% / 55%
C = 11% / 20%
D = 0% / 10%

On the other hand, during my time of working with Ciba Vision, the world-leading contact lens manufacturer, they preferred to classify the *potential business* on the basis of the number of new patients that an optometrist would fit with contact lenses every month.

Simple modification of the system will make it work in your business and allow us to address some of the other **strategic** considerations. When you have completed your classification system, insert into each box of the grid the number of customers in each classification. The first *strategic* consideration would be the objectives whenever calling on the various customers.

Refer back to your business MAP and in conjunction with your classifications, let's consider the following:

'CORE BUSINESS'

Whatever your classification, these would probably be in the A group for penetration, therefore some of your objectives would be:

1 To maintain your position and fight off any competition, perhaps by increasing your number of contacts within these accounts. Perhaps by involving other people and departments in your organisation with various levels within the customer's organisation.

This is called 'multi-level contact' and will be referred to again when we look at building customer loyalty.

2 To recognise the *product life cycles* in your business and create organic growth within these accounts by introducing new products or services, or working with the customer to solve potential problems.

3 To recognise the product life cycles in your business and delay the decline of your existing products for as long as possible, without damaging future selling opportunities.

At the end of this section I will give you a brief overview of product life cycles, for those of you who have not yet read any of the standard works on marketing.

REGULAR BUYING CUSTOMERS

Some of the objectives here would be:

1 To convert these to 'core business' by increasing your share of the potential business available and the introduction of new products and services.

69

2 To maintain and build upon your position during the various stages in the product life cycle.

INFREQUENT BUYERS

1 To convert these to regular buying customers, where possible, by building your share and improving your position, particularly with products or services which are in *growth*.

WORKING OPPORTUNITIES

1 To convert these to regular buying customers by the application of good quality selling skills.

Finally, you need to ask yourself where you should be spending your time.

I have worked with some companies who spent so much time calling on their existing customer base that there was little or often no time left to work on new business opportunities. There are situations where this is relevant, particularly if you're vulnerable in these accounts. However, many companies who become involved in this forget to identify whether they have a sales team of **hunters** or **farmers**.

Hunters are very good at winning new business and new customers and in fact this is how they get their buzz; making new conquests. For many of them it's part of the game that they play. *Farmers* are the people who hold on to and grow what they have, but usually don't like having to break new ground and are less comfortable in new situations.

There is a place in selling for both of these. Indeed, I know of one company in the UK that has two separate sales forces;

one of hunters to open the new accounts and another of farmers to keep them.

If you find it difficult identifying the hunters, here's a tip. They have usually been married more than once, and their current partner doesn't like them either!

It is possible to have a sales person who is both a hunter and a farmer, but these people are extremely rare and very few managers know how to handle them. However, whether you're a farmer or a hunter, or a mix of both, consider the amount of effort that you put into calling on your customers. Ask yourself the following:

1 How likely is it that by calling frequently on an F/A classification (a customer who has the potential to spend up to £2,999 and where your anticipated share of that is over 75 per cent), you will be able to grow that account into an E/A or even an E/B?
2 If you are calling on an A/B classification, how much competition will you find yourself up against?
3 Will it be easier to balance your short- and long-term results by aiming to increase your penetration with customers who are currently D/D?

These and many more are the types of question you should ask of yourself, before you plan your calls.

Product life cycles

In the points that I made earlier regarding the strategic considerations with the different customers, I referred to product life cycles. It may be appropriate at this point to give you an insight into product life cycles and some real-life examples of what can happen.

71

If you look at Figure 3.4, you will get an idea of how product life cycles affect us all.

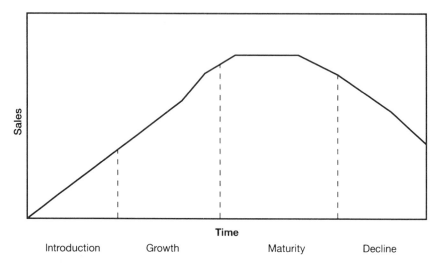

Fig 3.4 Product life cycles

Every product or service has a useful life, during which it goes through the classic stages from **Introduction** into **Growth**, then into **Maturity** and finally **Decline**. Of course, from product to product, this life cycle can have very different time spans. During the various stages, we have opportunities as sales people to take advantage of these when we consider how and to whom we should sell our products or services.

I was fortunate in the early 1970s to be working with Rank Xerox, selling the **only** plain paper copier on the market. I was also involved in the early days of commercial radio in the UK when I worked with Radio Clyde in Scotland. Both of these are splendid examples of working in areas of growth, in fact of rapid growth.

This will not always be the case for those of you reading this book. Some of you may very well be working in areas which are either in maturity or even decline. This doesn't mean to say that you shouldn't make strategic decisions regarding your objectives in either of these areas. The real danger in these areas is that a competitor may introduce a new product which takes your market away from you.

In the late 1960s and early 1970s there was a calculating device which was very popular among draughtsmen and engineers, called a slide rule. By the mid-1970s the development of pocket calculators had effectively put an end to the life of that product. This in itself regenerated a different market, that of portable power batteries.

Not *very* long afterwards, the introduction of solar power cells made a significant dent in this new market for batteries.

73

Similarly, the introduction of word processors has made a significant impact on the typewriter market. But, the life cycle of a product can be brought to a premature end for reasons which are not directly associated with competitive products. Look at how the reduction in the amount of people who smoke tobacco has meant a corresponding reduction in the demand for cigarette lighters.

The considerations for you as sales people must be:

1 If you are representing a major player in a given market, can you 'milk' that situation through maturity and decline? Bear in mind that it is unlikely that many new companies will decide to launch themselves into a market in either of those stages.

2 Is there some way in which your company can regenerate the life cycle of a product to arrest any decline and relaunch it back into growth?

How many times have detergent manufacturers and others created that type of situation, simply by repackaging?

3 If there is a new product development on the way, can your company be the one which effectively shortens the life cycle of one of its own products by launching its replacement?

If you check Figure 3.5, you will see that the 'dotted' line numbered '1' shows you what can happen to a regenerated product or that numbered '2', what happens when a new product shortens an existing product's life cycle.

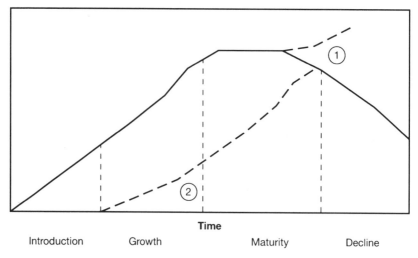

Time

Introduction   Growth   Maturity   Decline

(1) The effect of regenerating a product by making small improvements, repackaging, changing the colour, etc., or perhaps finding a new application and launching it on a different market

(2) Typically what happens when the introduction of a new product shortens the life cycle of an existing product

Fig. 3.5 Regenerating or shortening the life cycle of an existing product

This has only been a very small insight into the subject of product life cycles, but for those of you who would like to learn more, I would recommend that you read either: *Marketing Management* by Philip Kotler, or *Competitive Strategy* by Michael E Porter.

Setting priorities

You will need to discipline yourself to ensure that you work to your plan and that any change to that plan is justified by a higher priority.

Setting priorities is nothing more than evaluating the *return on your time invested*. Prioritising is the essence of good time management. Define your activities in three ways:

1 Things you **must** do today.
2 Things you **should** do today.
3 Things you **could** do today, but which are of lesser importance.

Don't ask yourself, 'Where am I going next week?', ask yourself, 'Where should I be going next week?'

So, how much time do you actually spend with your customers?

If you refer back to the action plan that we put together for the first three months of the year, you will recall that we only managed to have a total of 44 selling days over that period, and this could easily have been less. But, more importantly, within the selling days that *are* available, you will be amazed at how little time you actually spend 'face to face' with your customers!

Think about the time you spend during the day travelling between calls. Then think about the time you spend in waiting rooms, reception areas etc., before the customer gets round to seeing you – even with an appointment.

How often are you interrupted during your meeting with the customer? How often does the customer break the appointment without notice, leaving you to reschedule your plan? How much time do you spend bringing your customer records up to date after each call?

For the next few days, make a note of when you meet the customer, not when you arrive at the place of business, and when you part. Also make a note of any time taken up by interruptions. You will soon come to realise that your time with your customers is very limited, which makes it all the more important that you use that time effectively and that you put yourself in front of the right type of customer and prospect. So before we leave this chapter, let's spend a little time thinking about profiling our customers and prospects.

Profiling customers and prospects

Many of us frantically rush around our territories like headless chickens, yet there is a fairly simple solution to improving the direction of our activity. Go back over your existing customer base; the core business and the regular buying customers:

- What type of companies are they?
- What size?
- What businesses are they in?
- Why do they buy your products and services?
- Who are their customers?
- Who is your point of contact?
- What new developments are taking place within these companies?
- Who are their competitors?

You will find some distinct similarities that will enable you to target new prospective customers.

Also try to establish in your own mind the *real reasons* why your customers buy from you? You may have to indulge in a little lateral thinking, but consider the following:

1 People don't buy double glazing – they buy:

- Freedom from maintenance.

- Heat insulation.

- Noise reduction, etc.

2 People don't buy life insurance – they buy:

- Peace of mind.

- Future security for their families and dependants, etc.

77

3 People don't buy motors cars – they buy:

- Independence from public transport.

- The freedom to travel where and when they wish – usually in comfort

- Status and prestige, etc.

4 Anyone buying a product from you, which becomes a part of the product that they sell, doesn't buy your product – they buy:

- Their customers' satisfaction.

- The ability to make profit.

- The ability to remain and grow in business, etc.

5 People don't buy office-cleaning services – they buy:

- A clean and safe environment in which to work.

- A reduction in their own direct workforce.

- Freedom from the worries of managing staff holidays, sickness, etc.

When you can define the types of people who can buy from you and the real reasons why they buy, you will much more readily identify new prospects on whom it becomes effective to call.

Always remember that none of us **plan to fail**, but most of us **fail to plan**!

In my Introduction to this book, I referred to the KISS principle, i.e. Keep It Simple, Stupid. I also referred to the fact that sales people hate paperwork. Both statements, while true, were made to get a reaction. By virtue of the fact that you are still reading at this stage, it obviously worked. Let's put both of these together and try to create:

A KISS principle call reporting system

In putting this together you will probably have to secure the support of your sales manager or director in making any changes, but you might consider the effort to be worthwhile.

I worked with a company who had instituted a system whereby the sales report included such items as:

- The time of arrival at the call.
- The time when the customer or prospect actually saw you.
- The time when you left the call.
- The travelling time between that call and the next, etc.

I know that earlier in this chapter I have suggested, *for your own information*, that you occasionally keep track of the amount of time you spend face to face with your customers, but I think that if you have to include it in a call report it is a downright waste of everybody's time and effort! Why anyone would really want this information is beyond me, and the three questions I would ask are:

1 Does anybody read it?
2 Is the information accurate?
3 Is it used for any *meaningful* purpose, other than to beat the sales force over the head?

Ask yourself and your manager, what is the purpose of the call report? My experience is that the real purpose is to find out what activity has taken place, with whom and the outcome of that activity. So the information you will need is as follows:

1 *On whom did you call?*
   This will give the quantity of activity.
2 *Into which part of the Business MAP do they fit?*
   Is it a working opportunity (WO), an infrequent buyer (IB), a regular buying customer (RB) or core business (CB)? This will tell where your time is being spent and quickly indicate whether your direction of activity is on course.

   You will notice that I have omitted market opportunities (MO). This is because I believe that even if you have been unsuccessful in the first call, the fact that you had a meaningful call made it a working opportunity.

3 *Did you get an order?*
   You don't need any more detail, the order that arrives at the office gives all of that.

4 *If you didn't get an order, what probability of success figure have you applied to this customer or prospect?*

79

This allows for more accurate forecasting and serves as a double check that the call had a meaningful objective.

5 *Was it an appointment or non-appointment call?*
This will give an indication of how well you plan as well as the ratio between appointment and non-appointment calls.

6 *Is there a follow up appointment?*
This will indicate whether or not you are coming out of the call with anything concrete.

7 *What is the customer classification?*
This will give an indication of the direction of your activity.

There are seven items outlined above and with very few exceptions I doubt if there needs to be any more. In terms of reporting, other than the customer's or prospect's name, the rest is almost a 'tick list'.

Table 3.8 should help you to create the KISS principle call report.

You will see by looking at the table that it will take nanoseconds to complete a call report that has some real meaning and is therefore likely to be read. If you have to make any modifications to the table, take something out – don't add anything to it. Any other information needed will be supplied by other paperwork, e.g. the customer's order, your future call plan etc. Perhaps the next time a company is designing a call reporting system, they should ask the sales force – who are the ones who need to operate it!

In the next chapter we will look at how to get face to face with these prospects and customers.

Table 3.8 The KISS principle call report

Customer or Prospect	MAP	Order	Prob %	Appt.	F/up Appt.	Class'n
Name	WO or IB or RB or CB	'tick' or Y/N	80	'tick' or Y/N	Date of appt. or Y/N	B/C

SUMMARY

- Create a *meaningful action plan* by identifying the amount of selling time available to you.

- Set yourself *targets for activity* as well as results.

- Break these targets into stages and *monitor your success*

- Divide your territory into manageable 'chunks'.

- Create a *rolling five-week plan* around your appointments or your fixed schedule.

- *Classify your customers* and *identify the objectives* with each.

- Set *priorities* and stick to them to achieve a return of time invested.

- *Profile customers and prospects* to enable you to identify new business opportunities.

- Think about the *real reasons* why people buy from you.

- Sit down with your Manager and create a *KISS principle call reporting system.*

4

How to get Face to Face

Cold calling

Some of you will find in your businesses that cold calling is appropriate and others will find that it isn't. The real problems that I have with cold calling are:

- You usually won't know the name of the contact or the nature and size of the opportunity. In short, they are not yet market opportunities and this generally makes cold calling only another form of market research.

- Because you don't have the necessary information, you may not be as well prepared as you otherwise might.

- Cold calling is not nearly as professional as calling by pre-arrangement.

I'm sure that you have all, at some time or another, seen the signs on companies' reception doorways – on the outside,

> 'TRAVELLERS WILL ONLY BE SEEN BETWEEN 10 AND 12 ON TUESDAYS AND THURSDAYS'

Travellers! This smacks of the old Music Hall references to 'Travelling in Ladies Underwear', and there is nothing about that description that inspires any thoughts of professionalism. Even worse, is the awareness that notices in some bars in the Midlands of England refer to 'No Travellers' by which they mean gypsies and tinkers!

Hardly the type of image that any thinking manager would wish to associate with her or his sales force – but then again I have to admit that I believe that *thinking managers* are extremely thin on the ground. Believe it or not, I still know some companies who refer to their sales people as 'commercial travellers'. It conjures up an image of a marauding band of nomads, peddling their wares to all and sundry.

Horrifying, isn't it!

If you have to cold call, do so on the basis of 'researching' for information, which you can use at a later date. It may be that occasionally you will get the opportunity to speak to the person responsible and, if you're prepared, you could take advantage of that.

WHEN TO MAKE A COLD CALL

1 When you're in an area and have some free time; because an appointment has been cancelled at short notice; or perhaps a sales call didn't last as long as the time that you had allowed and you have no other identified market or working opportunities in that area – **YET!**

2 When you notice something new or unusual happening; e.g. a new business has opened up and you want to get some information on the business. Or, you see unusual activity around a particular business and want to investigate it further.

3 You have deliberately set aside time to walk over an area with a view to identifying some new market opportunities.

In the case of number 2, above, let me give you a couple of examples from my own past selling career.

Some years ago, I worked with the Exclusive Cleaning

Group, the large contract cleaning company, part of whose service was the cleaning of new or newly refurbished premises prior to the occupants moving in.

In these situations, we would investigate any new building or anywhere where there was major refurbishment taking place, and arrange to meet with the agent in charge of the site, so that we could submit a quote for the 'building clean'. During this, we were also able to discover the name of the company moving into the new premises, and were sometimes even able to get from the agent the name of the person responsible in that new company, for the management of the premises.

85

Another example from the same business, regarding unusual activity, was when there was an exceptionally large number of a competitor's vehicles outside an office or a shop – this would usually indicate a problem! Whenever anything was going wrong in that situation, supervisors and management were called in by the customer to sort out the problem – hence the number of vehicles at the customer's premises.

This meant an opportunity to sell.

I had the habit of leaving home very early in the morning and driving through the city centre, passing the major prospects in my area who were currently dealing with my competition, just to look for this type of activity. Most department stores and major retailers have their premises cleaned early in the morning before the day's business, so this was the time that there could be an indication that something was going wrong. It also meant that because of light traffic, I could carry out this exercise fairly quickly.

By the time that the office where I was based had opened for the day, I was already armed with the list of people that I wanted to contact with a view to setting up an appointment. If there had been a problem, they were invariably pleased to hear from me. Is there a similar type of 'early warning system' in your business?

In all other cases of cold calling, I was looking for the type of information that I outlined in the last chapter when we looked at profiling customers. The advantage of this form of research is that you can gain a great deal of information from the receptionist, secretary or simply from people working around the premises.

You can also observe a great deal, such as:

- Is there evidence of competitive equipment or goods around the area?
- Are there competitors' vehicles around the area?
- Does the business look prosperous?
- What kind of area is it in?
- Do the people look busy?
- Are there other sales people waiting in the reception or waiting room?

All of this information allows you to call later to make an appointment, knowing that you're armed with more information about the prospect's business than he or she is aware. However, the major disadvantage of this type of research is that it is extremely time consuming. Whereas, making an appointment:

- saves your time;
- saves your contact's time;

- is highly professional;

- gives you time to prepare for the meeting;

- gives your contact time to prepare for the meeting;

- enables you to ensure that you're dealing at the right level;

- should ensure that there are no interruptions to your meeting.

Cold calling for appointments

If you call in to the premises and don't have the information that you need, get it before you try to make the appointment. Having armed yourself with the information, try to get to talk to your contact or his or her secretary – *with a view to making the appointment*, nothing more. If you're unable to do this, at least you have enough information to make a telephone call later to set up the appointment.

The disadvantages of this situation are:

1 You may be asked to leave some information, literature etc., which will give your contact the opportunity to make a judgement about your product or service, in your absence.
2 You may be asked to make a presentation of your products or services on the spot – and you may not be prepared.

Making appointments by telephone

In all of the work that I carry out with sales people, this is the area where I find the greatest weaknesses and is the area that they hate the most!

Many years ago when I was a 'rookie' salesman with Rank

Xerox, I worked with one of the finest sales people it has ever been my pleasure to meet, Peter Chamberlain. Peter was, and I'm sure still is, the epitome of the ultimate sales person; professional, listening, polished, hard-working, empathic and thinking – but he hated making telephone calls to set up appointments. We worked an area as a two-man team and, while I was learning from him, I used to set up the appointments and he made the sales.

There are four very simple reasons why sales people hate making telephone appointments:

1 There is a limited amount of time to talk to the contact.
2 It is one of the few situations in which sales people very quickly have to offer the contact the opportunity to say **NO**!
3 There is no eye contact.
4 It is very easy to be dragged into a conversation about your product or service, with very little opportunity to gain enough information about the prospective customer to be able to make any kind of reasoned sale.

Yet, making appointments by telephone is the most efficient use of your time in this area of your activity. So let's take the bit between our teeth and see if we can structure an approach to this activity that will make it more successful for you, and therefore less stressful.

SOME GUIDELINES WHEN TELEPHONING FOR APPOINTMENTS

First I'll give you a list of guidelines, which then I'll expand on:

■ Plan and control your telephoning.

- Speak distinctly.
- SMILE!
- Be enthusiastic.
- Be alert.
- Be natural and reasonable.
- Know what you are going to say.
- Get impact early and arouse interest.
- Sell the appointment – don't sell the product.
- Keep asking for the appointment by giving alternatives

Planning and control

89

I wouldn't expect you to wander aimlessly around your territory hoping to get lucky, so why should your activity on the telephone be any different.

Speak distinctly

We live in a multi-cultural and cosmopolitan society where regional and national variations in our speech can cause difficulty with understanding. You also have to remember when using the telephone, that you do not have the advantage of being able to see the other party and are reliant purely on the senses of hearing and speech – and all of this presupposes that there is a clear telephone line in the first place!

In my own case, I have a very deep voice and a fairly pronounced West of Scotland accent. Plus, in keeping with most people from that part of the world, I have a tendency to speak very quickly. Whenever I am on the telephone, I have to remember to take a deep breath and speak more slowly and more clearly than I would normally in a face-to-face situation.

In fact, I have had situations where there were friends of mine in the same room while I was on the telephone, who could tell from my speech that I was in conversation with a fellow Scot – my accent and speed of delivery had altered so much! Finally, remember we all have 'telephone voices' – don't be embarrassed, use yours to good effect.

Smile!

The facial muscles you use to smile are such that they alter your voice. When you smile on the telephone, people can 'hear' the smile!

Would you rather speak to someone on the telephone who sounds happy or someone who sounds totally miserable?

Enthusiasm

If *you* can't be enthusiastic about the prospect of meeting with someone to discuss your products and services, *why should they*? In fact, why should they meet you at all? Remember that the expression 'monotonous' comes from the word 'monotone'. Vary your voice, don't speak in a monotone and you won't sound monotonous.

Alertness

You have limited time on the telephone, be alert for little signals which improve your chances of getting the appointment. Sales people are usually very alert to opportunities in face-to-face situations, and it's every bit as important on the telephone.

Being natural and reasonable

Have you noticed how the character and behaviour of some people change the minute that they find themselves behind the wheel of a car? They become totally unreasonable and aggressive. I have observed very similar behaviour on the telephone. It's almost as if the fact of there being no face-to-face contact allows them to become entirely different 'animals'. *Be yourself* – for no other reason except that when you do come face to face with your prospect, they will notice the difference.

I recall a number of years ago telephoning to make an appointment with the managing director of a very large engineering company. Having extreme difficulty in getting his secretary to fit me in to his appointment schedule, I became so 'pushy' that I eventually got the appointment.

When I had finished my call, and taken a couple of minutes to reflect on how the call had gone I realised that I had not only been 'pushy', I had been downright *rude*!

Bearing in mind the power that many secretaries wield, it occurred to me that I may very well have gained the appointment, but I had certainly not won a 'friend' in that MD's secretary. I took a deep breath and called back to speak to the secretary. When we were connected I explained that in my eagerness to make an appointment with the MD, I had been rude to her and had called back to apologise.

At this point, much to my surprise, she sprang to my defence and assured me that I had in no way been rude or unpleasant to her. After a few more moments of conversation, I was able to finish the telephone call feeling that I had corrected a potentially troublesome situation. When the time for my appointment came around it was carried out very successfully, but I shudder to think about the reception I could have had, if I hadn't made the second phone call.

Know what you're going to say

Don't make it up as you go along. Be prepared; have your standard introduction to hand and sound professional and natural.

Get impact early

When you telephone for an appointment, you are competing with all of the other things that occupy your contact's time. If you want that contact to give up time to see you, you have to say something that will interest her or him, early in your conversation, to even get the time to try to make the appointment.

Sell the appointment – don't sell the product

Unless you are in 'telephone selling', never sell your product on the telephone. The objective of the phone call is to create enough interest for the prospect to want to spend time with you, discovering about your products and services. So, only give enough information to motivate the prospect to want to see you.

Keep asking for the appointment – by giving alternatives

When faced with the kind of time limitations that you experience in telephone calls, limit the number of decisions that the prospect has to make. The decision should not be about whether or not to see you, but about *when*! Ask for the appointment frequently, and keep giving alternative times so that it is about the choice of the alternatives only that the prospect has to decide.

Creating your own telephone script

I told you earlier that you would need to know what you are going to say. My experience is that the best way to make sure that you don't mumble or stumble over what you want to say is to have it written down in front of you. Make it large, **bold** print – you need to be able to see it clearly in order that you can read it and make it sound natural and not scripted.

A further point I would make about telephoning is: whenever possible, do it *standing up!*

There are two reasons for this:

1 When you are in an upright position your voice sounds clearer. If you're sitting slouched, it comes across over the telephone.
2 When you're standing up, you think faster and are more alert.

93

I have a small portable drawing-board that I use, with my introduction placed on it, and I literally walk around the room while I am speaking on the telephone. It really does improve my ability to 'think on my feet'.

There are several ways of – Getting hold of the MAN.

Let me explain that this is not a sexist remark; it is the standard acronym that we use in selling to identify the proper contact, i.e. **Money, Authority and Need**.

The first way is to be *assumptive*, e.g. 'Good morning, Robert Smith please'.

You will often find that this type of approach is such that the receptionist or secretary will assume that you know Robert Smith and therefore increase the chance of your being connected without further delay.

Another way is to be *polite and requesting*. 'Could you put me through to Mr Smith, please?'

Or, if you don't know the name of the contact, 'Good morning, I wonder if you could help me? Could you tell me the name of the senior partner/managing director/office equipment buyer, please?'

Whenever I have had to use the latter of these two requests, I prefer to get the information and call back another day, when I can go straight into the *assumptive*. I usually find that obtaining this information is not difficult, but in any event, **don't tell the receptionist or secretary who you are until you are asked**.

In addition, try not to discuss your business or the reason for your call, with the receptionist or secretary. However, if you have to say anything, give a little – **not a lot**.

The above approaches may seem cold and calculating to you, and some of you may even think that they border on being rude, but let me explain. I mentioned earlier the *power* that secretaries have. One of the facts of life that you will have to face is that secretaries and receptionists can be very powerful people. There are two major reasons why this power comes about:

1 They are *given* this power by weak managers.
2 They *assume* this power, and either it isn't noticed or weak managers do notice – and then do nothing about it.

The point is that they often have power beyond their capabilities!

I have spent enough time trying to speak to people, being balked by secretaries and receptionists, to know that if I wanted to make an appointment with the secretary or receptionist, I would be calling them in the first place and not their respective bosses! If they had the real power to make the decisions, I would be happy to meet with them, but invariably they haven't so why should they be placed between me and the 'decision maker' as a buffer?

As I write this book, I cannot help but think of two specific situations which are current in my own business. I have begun working with a subsidiary of a large conglomerate where my presence has been at the invitation of a member of the Board of Directors.

In calling to speak to directors of this company, and in waiting in reception on prearranged appointments, I have witnessed the behaviour of one of the rudest receptionists I have seen in over 25 years. Yet no one seems to notice that this young lady has a serious attitude problem.

There is another situation in the South of England where I have been trying, for some considerable time, to make contact with the managing director of a subsidiary of a 'household name', multi-national corporation. However, his secretary seems to be running the business and I don't think he even knows that I exist! Paradoxically, in my business, the more that this situation prevails, the more they need the services of someone like me.

I'm certainly not the first person to recognise this problem. In 1970, Robert Townsend – former Chairman of Avis Rent-A-Car Corporation, wrote a book entitled *Up The Organisation*.

In the chapter; 'Freedom From a Secretary', he says, after he had decided to do without a secretary:

An important thing I learned was that my secretary had been acting like an assistant-to. Helping me where I didn't want and couldn't be helped. Playing favourites with my associates. I got much closer to the people who reported to me when I didn't have a buffer state outside my office.

He also says in an earlier chapter of the same book, 'try calling yourself up and see what indignities you've built into your own defences'.

This may not be much comfort for those of you who are trying to make appointments and finding difficulty with secretaries and receptionists, but if you are a manager or a director reading this at present, think about what I've said and if you don't believe me, call me up and I'll give you the names of some of the most successful people in Commerce and Industry who don't have this problem, because they recognise that it can exist.

I do need to make the point that to the best of my knowledge, none of the situations I have described here fall into that other category of gaining power; the power granted to a secretary or receptionist from the bedroom!

If I ever get around to writing those stories, I would need to do so within a work of fiction to protect myself from libel legislation. Believe me, it would be a much longer book than this one!

That aside, good companies recognise that the first impression any potential customer has about their organisation is the voice which answers the telephone. They want that impression to be a good one. So bearing that in mind, what do you do when confronted by a rude receptionist or secretary?

The short answer is that you ask pleasantly, but with a convicted firmness in your voice, 'could you tell me who I'm speaking to please?' Remember, most people who are being rude know it. In fact some of them revel in it. However, they probably don't want their bosses to realise it. So, implicit in that question should be the idea that you may decide to complain about their attitude. After all you have absolutely nothing to lose. If, however, you can't get past a rude receptionist or secretary, you may as well take your activity elsewhere.

Sometimes, it is not simply a case of being confronted by rudeness, but simply a case of a secretary or receptionist being over zealous of her boss's health, and/or sanity. So what do you do when the receptionist or secretary uses the 'He'll ring you back' ploy. It could be that the offer to have your call returned is genuine, but it may be simply a put-off, so try this. 'Thank you, I realise that Mr Smith is a very busy man, so if he hasn't managed to get back to me by 3 o'clock, I'll call him back myself.'

Robert Townsend also explains in *Up The Organisation*, what he did after he had disposed of the use of a secretary.

> 'The **Telephone Operators** took all my calls until eleven in the morning saying, "May I have Mr Townsend call you back?". Then at eleven, they'd send all the call messages in, start putting incoming calls through, and I would do the dialling myself. Result: nobody mad. (Note, no offence because when she offers to have me call back, she hasn't asked who you are.)'

In the quotation above, the emphasis on telephone operators is mine not Robert Townsend's, because I wanted to make the difference between them and receptionists. I have yet to meet a rude telephone operator. The reason being that, telephone operators are much less likely to suffer from delu-

97

sions of grandeur with respect to their positions of power. I use the expression 'delusions of grandeur' here, when in fact whenever I am running training programmes, I more accurately refer to this as *delusions of adequacy*.

If I may digress for a moment, I have a 'tip' which you may find useful when you have finally secured an appointment in spite of the attempts of the rude receptionist.

I recall a situation some time ago when I was working with Daryl Street, who was, at the time, one of the field sales executives of Ciba Vision. As we were driving to one of his appointments he was telling me about the difficulty he had encountered in getting past a very rude receptionist in one of the optical practices which he had targeted for a new product. Such is the apparent power of some of these people that he was genuinely concerned about the reception he would get from her when he arrived.

I suggested to him that instead of announcing on his arrival that he had an appointment with the optometrist or that he was expected, he should say, 'Mr Smith asked me to call to see him at 3.00 o'clock!'. If I tell you that as soon as he said that he was given the 'red carpet' treatment by the receptionist, I would only be guilty of the mildest over-statement.

In case you think that my recommendation bordered on 'poetic licence', the truth of the matter is that when someone agrees to see you at a given time, they have effectively asked you to call to see them at that time.

I dare you to use it – because it works!

However, let me continue. If you have finally managed to get through to the MAN, be prepared for what you want to say.

Use the following as a guideline for writing your own telephone scripts.

CONTACTING MARKET OPPORTUNITIES

'Good morning Mr Smith, my name is Mary Finn from (your company). We are the (use an interest 'grabber' here) . . . I'd like to make an appointment to introduce myself and discuss the range of my company's products and how they may be of benefit to you in your business. I will be in Bristol next Monday, would 10 o'clock in the morning suit or would you prefer the afternoon?'

Note: I refer to an interest 'grabber'. There must be one for your company and business, such as:

- We are at the leading edge of technology in . . .
- We are the local specialists in . . .
- We are the world leaders in . . . etc.

Create a good interest 'grabber', it will improve your chances of being given a hearing.

CONTACTING INFREQUENT BUYERS

'Good morning Mrs Brown, my name is Simon Green of (your company). While I know that you occasionally use some of our products, I would like to make an appointment to see you, to talk about our other products and their possible suitability in your business. I will be in Manchester next Monday and Tuesday, which day would be most convenient for you? Would you prefer the morning or the afternoon?'

CONTACTING REGULAR BUYING CUSTOMERS TO INTRODUCE A NEW PRODUCT

'Good morning John, it's Jane Smith here from (your company). At various times in the past, we've discussed the different products in our range and you may have heard that we've introduced (the new product or service). I would like to make an appointment with you so that we could discuss this in some detail. I'll be in Edinburgh on Monday and Thursday, which day would suit you best? Would you prefer early in the morning or late in the afternoon?'

I haven't included the other ranges of possibilities where you will telephone for an appointment, which would include:

- Telephoning your core business – you should be so well known to them that it's like calling an old friend.

- Telephoning your working opportunities – you shouldn't need to do this, because with working opportunities you should have booked the return appointment at your previous meeting – **always**!

However, in your normal working situation you may encounter resistance when trying to make appointments. I would suggest that in most of these circumstances you have failed to get the prospect's interest, and while it may be addressing the symptom rather than the disease, listed below are some of the most common objections I have come across when trying to make appointments, together with some ways of overcoming these.

The thing you have to remember is not to get pulled into discussing your products or services on the telephone, but to sell the appointment.

Ways to overcome certain objections

Objection:

Send me literature

Answer:

I'd be pleased to send you literature, but I would prefer to deliver it personally so that I can explain it and answer any questions you may raise. I would also like to explain how (the product) has been successful in other businesses. Would Tuesday at 2.00 o'clock be convenient or would you prefer later at 4.00?

Or

I'll certainly send you literature so that you have some idea of how (the product) works. Perhaps we could arrange an appointment now so that I can come along and explain it in some detail and answer any questions you may raise having read it? Would Monday at 8.30 be suitable or would you prefer Wednesday at 11.00?

Or (if it's TRUE)

The nature of our business is such that we don't produce standard literature, but if after ten minutes I haven't said anything of interest I'll be happy to leave. So can we say Thursday at 12.00 or Friday at 10.00?

Objection:

It would be better if you saw . . .

(someone else – usually an assistant or someone less senior in the company)

Answer:

Yes, I understand that and it may well be that he or she can provide some valuable information when we meet. However, at this stage it would be good to see you first as the person in authority, responsible for introducing new ideas into your business. So would Tuesday at 10.00 be OK or would you prefer later in the day around 3.00?

Objection:

I'm not interested

Answer:

I can appreciate that you may not be interested in something that I haven't had the chance to fully explain yet. However, if after ten minutes you're still not interested in what other people have been getting out of using (the product), I'll leave. So how about Tuesday at 9.00 or would it be better on Thursday at 2.30?

Objection:

Tell me about it now

Answer:

I'd like to, but I would need to relate the use of (the product) to the particular situation in your business, so would Thursday at 9.30 be OK or would you prefer next Monday at 5.00?

Objection:

Your company is too expensive

Answer:

I believe that's a popular misconception Mrs Brown, and obviously at the moment I'm unable to talk about relative costs as we could be talking about an individual service and a complete package. However, a ten minute discussion would establish whether what we have to offer could be of benefit to you. So is Tuesday at 11.00 convenient or would you prefer Wednesday at 3.15?

Objection:

103

You would be wasting your time

Answer:

I wouldn't consider it a waste of my time or yours if I was able to give you some information on our range of products or services which could be of value to you, if not now, at some time in the future. So would Monday at 9.30 suit you or would it be better on Thursday at 4.00?

Objection:

I already use (a competitor)

I realised that may be the case and it's one of the reasons for my call. With your experience of (the competitor), you will be in a perfect position to evaluate the benefit of our total package, which has been successfully introduced into other businesses similar to your own. Would Monday at 10.15 be suitable or would you prefer later in the afternoon?

Objection:

I already use (a competitor) and we are under contract until the end of this year

Answer:

I appreciate that and it's not an uncommon situation these days, Mr Smith. However, at the time when the contract comes up for renewal you will no doubt be very busy evaluating the alternatives which are available. A short meeting now would let you know if what we have to offer could come under consideration at that time. So would Monday at 11.15 be convenient or would it be better later in the day?

Objection:

We used your company before and had a bad experience

Answer:

I understand that Mrs Brown, and it's one of the reasons for my call. A great deal has happened since you last did business with us on a regular basis and what I'd like to do is bring you up to date on the most recent developments so that at some time in the future you may consider doing business with us again. Would Friday at 1.30 be OK or would you prefer earlier in the morning?

Objection:

I'm too busy

Answer:

Of course I realise that you're very busy Mr Smith, which is precisely why I telephoned to make an appointment. If we can agree on a time, then within ten minutes you will know if (the product) is going to be of sufficient value to allow further time or arrange a further meeting. Would Monday at 12.00 be OK or would it be easier for you after 5.00?

Objection:

We don't see the need for your type of product

Answer:

I can appreciate what you're saying Mrs Brown, it's a situation which I've experienced with others in the past. What I'd really like to do is not only discuss the various merits of (your product) but also explain the total package, and perhaps be able to relate the experiences of other businessmen whose *original thinking* was similar to your own. Would Thursday at 10.00 be convenient or would you prefer Friday, late afternoon?

105

Use the answers to the objections that I have given above and rewrite them, using your own words, but remember that we seldom write as we speak so you will have to practice your answers until such time as they sound perfectly natural.

When you are making appointments on the telephone there is a definite sequence to be followed to gain the maximum results, as follows:

The telephone appointment sequence

Use the following procedure:

- Give a polite, friendly greeting and identify yourself.

- Give the prospect enough information to arouse interest.

- Ask for the appointment, offering an alternative.

- Deal with any objections.

- Keep asking for the appointment.

- When you've been successful, restate the time and date of the appointment in your 'good-bye' remarks.

All of the above will improve your strike rate when making appointments, but remember that you will never win them all – even if you're selling genuine £50 notes for £1, there will always be someone who won't believe you – *including me*!

My own experience of trying to make appointments on the telephone is such that I reckon after the third objection to the appointment, you're not going to succeed – so put it down to experience and call someone else.

Some time ago, however, I had an experience on the telephone which caused me to break my three-objections rule. I had been given a reference to contact the local branch manager of Royal Life Insurance from the local branch manager of Abbey Life Insurance, with whom he had once worked.

From the first point of contact on the telephone there was a great deal of banter coming from the Royal Insurance manager. He began to feed me some of the 'classic' objections which I've outlined above and I was replying with those answers which I've given you. The tone of the call was not only friendly it was full of downright 'jollity'.

I handled the first three objections which were thrown at me and a fourth came along. Such was the tone of voice that I carried on going. Just about the time that I was close to exhausting my repertoire, the prospect said to me, 'That is a really good script you're using!' whereupon the only thing I could think to say was, 'Thank you very much, I think you'll find that the major difference between me and your own sales people is that I write my own scripts!'.

Well, be fair, I had nothing left to lose.

The reply came back, 'In that case I had better see you'.

Finally, some useful tips when telephoning for appointments:

- Don't make appointments on an 'ad hoc' basis.
- Set aside some quiet time:
  - If this is **in the office** – tell other people so that you won't be disturbed.
  - If this is **at home** – again tell other people. Don't have your husband or wife or friends calling you because they think when you're at home you're having the day off!
  - **In the car** – pull into a car park or some other quiet place. You can't concentrate with traffic rushing past you every few seconds. Also, don't call while mobile – even using the 'hands free' device. You won't be able to concentrate on the conversation and live as well!
  - If this is **in an hotel** – get into a quiet corner where you have room to work. Don't use a coin box – use a credit card or a telephone charge card or some other method which will not have your conversation interrupted by the disconnecting tone!
- Be prepared and have everything to hand:
  (i) your prospect and customer lists;

(ii) the contact names;

(iii) their telephone numbers;

(iv) any back up information you might need about them.

■ Organise yourself:

(i)   have your coffee or tea, take a comfort break etc;

(ii) have a standard confirmation system;

(iii) keep a separate phone call file.

Monitor your *Efforts and Success Rate* – using the form I gave you in chapter 3, which is headlined as follows;

Phone Calls made	Appointments gained	Failure at Secretary or Receptionist	Failure at Prospect or Customer	Objections encountered

SUMMARY

■ **The true professionals among us work by appointment.**

■ **The telephone is the best and most time and cost effective method of making appointments.**

■ **Prepare yourself by creating your own telephone script and devising an interest 'grabber'.**

■ **If you encounter objections on the telephone make sure that you have developed the best way to overcome these.**

■ **Monitor your success rate on the telephone and practise to improve it.**

5

Efficient working in the field

Now that you are more effective – you need to become more efficient.

The mobile office

THE CONTENTS OF YOUR CAR

Almost all of the sales people I have ever met had a number of things in common, not least of which was their disorganised chaos in respect of the amount of material they carried in their cars:

- At least one briefcase – not to be taken into the customer's premises, usually one of the airline pilot variety.

- A couple of boxes of various customer records and files.

- Samples and literature of various descriptions, much of it out of date.

- Old diaries – some going back many years.

- Computer printout of previous month's and year's business.

- The real briefcase *which can be taken into the customer* and the genuine up-to-date samples, literature and customer records and files.

- This is in addition to personal paraphernalia like golf clubs, children's seats, squash and /or tennis kit, football kit etc.

Small wonder so many of them opted for vehicles of the estate car variety. *They would have been better off using small trucks!*

The two questions I would like you to ask of yourself are:

1 What would happen to your business if your car was stolen?
2 What would happen if the contents fell into the hands of a competitor?

It hardly bears thinking about!

The difference between the mobile office and the one you have at home or at your office base is that the mobile office should only carry what you could possibly need today. So let's think about what you need today:

1 All of the personal stuff like golf clubs, squash kit etc., in case you have a cancelled appointment and can't be bothered doing any non-appointment calls or researching for market opportunities by cold calling or visiting the library!
2 The customer records and files you will need for today's field of operation, which can be readily identified by referring back to your rolling five-week plan.
3 The samples and literature you could need for the area in which you're working **Today** (all of them up to date).
4 Any other equipment you may need, like tape measures, torches etc.
5 The customer records you need for your company.
6 The briefcase that *you can take into the customer*, containing:

    (i)   order forms, if you use them, otherwise some other way of gaining the commitment to the business or reporting such back to your company;

(ii)   an up-to-date diary – so that you can book return appointments.

(iii)   Your rolling five-week plan so that you know when you will be back in the area;

(iv)   the quotations or correspondence relating to that customer;

(v)   your own private customer record card (of which more later in this chapter);

(vi)   a pen so that you can take notes and get the customer to sign orders;

(vii)   business cards – don't keep them in a pocket, they not only become 'dog eared', they become miniature note pads and one day you'll hand a business card to a customer with something completely inappropriate written on the back;

(viii)   in addition, for those of you who read *The Ultimate USP is You*, you will know that you also need your product analyses, objection files and 'digging for gold' and 'stages of the sale' reminders.

111

Your private customer records

All of the sales people with whom I work agree that it is usually easier to hold on to the customers they already have than to constantly have to find new business. They also agree that the key to this is building a long-term relationship with those customers. Yet, they almost invariably fail to recognise that *customers are real people too*!

Here's a small test for you.

Take a piece of paper and write down the names of your contacts within your top ten customers. Now alongside each name, write the following details:

- What they like to be called.
- When they celebrate their birthday.
- The name of their spouse.
- His or her birthday.
- How many children they have.
- Their birthday(s).
- Your contact's hobbies and leisure interests.
- How good they are at these various activities.
- If they are youth leaders, golf club secretaries, bridge club treasurers etc.

112

- Where they went on holiday last year.
- Where they are going on holiday this year.
- What type of holiday it is.
- Where they live.
- What kind of house it is.

I could go on for some considerable time, but implicit in such a test is the question, 'How much do you know about this person with whom you are trying to build a relationship?' I would also ask you how well you can build such a relationship if you don't know anything about the real person?

During the time that you're talking to customers about the business there is always some degree of social intercourse between you. Why not make a note of it? You should have a private record card for each of your major and regular customers. You should keep this with you when you call and you should remind yourself of the details before you make the call.

You can't be expected to remember everything, so write it down. If you are the only sales person calling on that customer who treats her or him as if they were real people, trust me, you will be the one getting the business! Keep a 6" x 4" (152mm x 101mm) file card for each customer with as much information on it as you can pick up – without interrogating the customer about her or his private life. The information will be there – you only have to listen.

Creating your own diary system

Believe it or not, I have recently come across some sales people who didn't permanently carry diaries. I even came across some who thought that their diaries should be provided by the company. This makes about as much sense as expecting the company to supply your underwear!

Your diary is an *important tool of your trade*, so get one that suits you and **always** have it with you.

So what type of diary should you have?

I have always favoured the loose-leaf type of personal organiser which is available from almost all of the large stationery retailers, but I have also found that the standard slim version isn't large enough for everything that I want to do with it, so I have opted for the larger A5 size.

Your life will be made much easier towards the end of the year if you can insert the early months of the following year instead of having two diaries to cope with the 'roll over' from this year to next. Also, I have found that the next year's diary is quite often not readily available until shortly before the new year begins.

On the other hand, you could always make a few notes on the back of your business cards and hope that you don't hand the one with an important appointment to one of your other customers.

Another advantage is that you can clear out the old months on a regular basis, keeping down the physical bulk of your diary – as well as creating space to insert notepaper. You don't have to discard the old months, file them away in the office in case you ever need to refer back to them.

Now that you have your loose-leaf diary, don't buy a complete package of standard stationery to put in it. Look around at the various types of insert which are available and choose the one that will suit the way you conduct your business. If you make several appointments a day, get the stationery that breaks each day down into one hour or half hour periods. This being the case, you will probably also want a diary insert that gives you one page for every day.

Stationery which allows you to overview either the whole year or a complete month, is very useful. I personally use both of these, but, on the other hand, I don't use the page-per-day type stationery because it's inappropriate to my business.

The first thing to do is take the year or month overview pages and blank out the days you know you will not be working; statutory holidays, annual holidays etc. Second, you can refer back to your five-week rolling plan and using either the overviews or the page per day, block out any days where you have to attend sales meetings, training seminars etc. These are also days when you won't be calling on customers.

Thirdly, with the remainder, make a note of the area in which you intend to work on each of the available remaining days, together with any fixed appointments you already have.

As you update your five-week plan, update your diary pages. Whatever you do, don't forget to make a note of important birthdays, such as your partner in life. I met a manager on a training programme about 12 years ago who had forgotten his wife's birthday – he's still paying for it.

Finally, make sure that you have a set of indexed telephone pages. It can be a real bind filling these in at the beginning, but after that they will be easy to keep up to date. Remember, unlike conventional diaries, you won't have to rewrite them every year.

115

Some of you may be working with a secretary or assistant who helps you manage your diary and keeps an office bound copy. Make sure that both diaries are always in agreement. If you make an appointment, make sure that it's logged in the office diary and similarly if an appointment is made for you, make sure that you note it in your personal one.

'COMPUTERISED' DIARIES AND SOFTWARE

The pace at which technology is moving is such that whatever I write in this section may very well be obsolete before the book is printed, so I'll try to stick to some principles which I believe will apply whatever the hardware or software that you use.

You may be using or thinking of using one of the following:

- A personal computer (PC).
- A laptop; basically a portable PC.

- A notebook; similar to the laptop, these are typically the size of a sheet of A4 paper and weigh around three kilogrammes.

- A subnotebook; about the size of this book and weighing around one kilogramme.

- A palmtop; as the name suggests, these are even smaller still and at the time of writing, appear to be becoming increasingly popular.

- A personal digital assistant; this is a fairly recent development in hand-held devices which combine computing power with good communications capabilities.

However, whatever the hardware or software, I think that before you make your choice you should ensure the following:

1 The hardware you are using should be able to be connected, directly or by modem, to a printer or a home/office based computer, so that you can download your computerised diary. You may find it an advantage to be able to refer to a back up of what you have planned and, as I mentioned before, you may wish to use a master diary so that others can make appointments on your behalf.
2 The software you are using should be able to print out in the format that you would use for your normal diary, whether this is personal organiser size, A5 or A4.

All of the major manufacturers, and many less well known, have a range of hardware from which you will be able to find something which suits your own purposes and which is within your company's or your own price range. The potential problem associated with the cost of these may very well mean, however, that to justify them you may need to use the hardware for more than just your diary system. I have at least one client who uses laptops which are modem linked to an office based computer for the purposes of transmitting call reports, call plans and orders from customers. It also produces the diary and is linked to electronic mail, thereby justifying the cost.

As far as software is concerned there are a number of specialised packages available from the very simple to the extremely complex. Basically the package which you choose should be dictated by your computer literacy and the hardware, including printing facilities, which you have available to you.

In recent times there have been a number of word processing packages launched which include diaries within the styles available and these are worthy of investigation. Whatever you choose, you need to be able to create a loose-leaf diary set up, so that you can print, on a regular basis, the updated diary pages that you use. This will enable you to minimise on the paperwork that you carry around with you and will help you ensure your personal organisation.

117

I still haven't found a busy sales person who was able to totally replace their conventional 'hard copy' diary system with the computerised diary, whatever the format.

ELECTRONIC MAIL

Many of the companies with whom I work have very sophisticated electronic mail systems, yet few of them provide the sales people who are tied in to that system with the ability to print what they have received.

I'm not suggesting for a minute that you would need to produce a printout of memos etc., sent to you by colleagues or managers, but if you use electronic mail, you need to have someone, somewhere, to supply you with a print out of your diary, otherwise the system is not being used to maximum advantage.

Mobile telephones, and the alternatives

Since the advent of mobile and portable telephones we find ourselves in a world of instant communication. However, maybe we need to take a step back and ask ourselves if this is really necessary or desirable. The problem with the mobile telephone is that you could find yourself with 'no hiding place' at all, and I firmly believe that there are times when you need to be able to get some peace and quiet, even if it's just to give you some thinking time.

118

There are some people, however, who feel the need to be in constant communication with someone – in many cases, any-one. The most ridiculous sight I have witnessed in recent years was at London's Heathrow Airport, when I saw a man pushing a fully laden baggage trolley through Terminal One while on the telephone. Trust me, nobody was ever that busy, that they couldn't even stop to make or take the call!

However, the portable telephone can be an absolute boon for someone like me who runs a small business. It's also wonderful for companies to be able to relay important and some-times urgent messages to their people, particularly field sales people.

So if the portable telephone is a 'value added' item to your business, think about the best way in which you can use it. Question whether it is more important to be able to receive incoming messages or make outgoing calls?

If the messages should be incoming, perhaps you should consider the low call tariff whereby the line rental is less but the outgoing call charges are higher. If the need is to make outgoing calls, then you should consider the standard tariff where the line rental is higher but the outgoing call charges less.

You also need to consider whether you should be calling in to the office on a regular basis or whether they should be calling you.

A few years ago I had the situation when working with one of my clients whereby the sales manager had instructed his field sales people to phone in to the office and have them call the sales people back to relay any messages etc. When I informed him that it was much more expensive to call a mobile telephone than it was to call from a mobile telephone, which was true at that time, he asked me not to make an issue of that point with the other managers. When I asked him why, he replied, 'The cost of the mobile telephone calls comes out of my budget for running the sales force, whereas the cost of calls from the office comes out of someone else's budget'.

When that happens, you know that the lunatics have truly taken over the asylum!

However, let's return to the primary purpose of having the mobile telephone.

INCOMING CALLS AND MESSAGES

What is the most cost-effective way of achieving this? Is it the mobile or portable telephone or is it better to use an electronic pager of some description? – particularly one which gives you a read out of the message as opposed to simply having you call in to your office to discover the message.

In any event, if you have a portable telephone try to remember that it can be switched off, particularly when you go into a customer's office. Woe betide anyone who visits my office and whose telephone begins to ring during our meeting! Leave the telephone in the car and call in to the office when you return from your meeting. Better still, have one that let's you know that there has been a call in your absence or that has an answering machine facility.

OUTGOING CALLS AND MESSAGES

With a few rare exceptions I can see no point in having a portable telephone unless you use it for outgoing calls, yet I have at least one client who having issued the sales force with mobile telephones has also issued the instruction that they are not to be used for outgoing calls.

Among the advantages of the mobile or portable telephone for making outgoing calls is the situation where a laptop computer can be modem linked to the office based computer via the mobile telephone. Another is the ability to arrange a quiet half hour during the day and make telephone calls to secure appointments. Yet another is to be able to make telephone calls when it is difficult to locate public telephones, particularly in rural areas, or to locate them in quiet areas without traffic thundering close by.

But are there more cost effective ways of handling some of these, and other, situations?

1 Is it necessary to transmit that information from your laptop to the office based computer during the day or would it be as effective to do it in the evening from home? Indeed, is

the reception from your mobile telephone to the main computer such that the information is accurately transmitted in the first place?

2 Can you organise yourself such that you can get a quiet half hour in an hotel somewhere to make your telephone calls in a less cramped environment than your car?

3 Is it cheaper to use a telephone card, or a telephone or other credit card to make these calls?

4 How often do you have to make telephone calls during the day at all?

Only you will know the answer to these questions in your situation and I am certainly not arguing against mobile or portable telephones, but I would question the way in which they are often used. If I find myself on board one more aircraft where some arrogant idiot has to be told by the cabin crew to switch off the telephone, I will scream!

121

In helping you become more efficient, there are many hi-technology solutions available today and I believe firmly that these should be used. However, I have found that in all too many situations these are imposed with so little thought that they create more problems than the advantages which they provide. Let me relate just such a situation.

I had a client a number of years ago who decided that in order to make the most effective use of the time available to the field sales force, they would invest in laptop computers which would be modem linked by car telephone to the main computer back at headquarters.

A wonderful idea, which unfortunately took no account of the fact that the field sales force were computer illiterate.

Simple solution; give the field sales force the necessary

training in computer skills! This would have been a great idea, if they had made sure that the person giving the training knew how to carry out training. As it was, he was simply a member of the IT department who was such an accomplished and gifted IT professional (no sarcasm here at all!), that he didn't speak the same language as the rest of us and didn't know how to communicate his ideas in layman's terms!

Eventually this problem was overcome by handing the training over to a member of the sales management team who happened to be extremely computer literate and was able to put together a very comprehensive and easily understood programme which developed the skills which were required.

122

On the day that everything was organised – the software in place on the laptops, the sales force trained in their use, the mobile telephones in place and the modems installed – everything was ready to go. But, that was the day that they discovered that the person who had been given the responsibility of negotiating a highly-competitive package for the purchase of some £30,000 worth of laptop computers had done an excellent job – except that the laptops which had been purchased were incompatible with the main computer!

Notwithstanding the cost, I am sure that you can begin to imagine the amount of time that was wasted in the whole exercise to achieve absolutely nothing.

Continuing on my theme of efficiency and effectiveness, many of you reading this book will find yourselves in the situation where you will either be working totally from home or you will be having to manage a great deal of your activity from home. Therefore I would like to address the next section to those situations.

Working from home

Most people are totally unaware of the fact that working from home is entirely different to working from an office.

In fact I have met a number of sales people who were quite simply unable to come to terms with working from home when they had previously spent their entire sales careers working from an office base. Much of this was due to the fact that no one had spelled out the differences and given them any guidelines.

When you work from an office base, at some point in most days you will arrive at the office, meet up with other people, have a coffee and a chat and generally feel a part of the organisation.

In current times it is even more common than before for sales people to work from their own homes, appearing at the office only on occasions such as meetings, training sessions etc. Now, one of the major talents that a sales person has is the ability to get on with others – we loosely refer to them as our social skills. The paradox is, that having been recruited with this in mind, we are then sent away to work from our own homes with few friendly faces, outside of our own family and social circles, with whom to communicate.

If you then add to that the fact that like most other professions we have our own language and our own culture, is it any wonder that our family and friends occasionally find that we bore them by talking about our work? *We are desperately trying to find someone else who understands what we go through on a day to day basis.*

HANDLING ISOLATION

There is only one sure way to handle isolation – **don't let yourself become isolated!** Try to:

- Telephone the office at least once a day and speak to as many different people as you can so that you begin to feel like one of the group.

- Make a point of getting in touch with colleagues outside of business hours – just for a chat about the kind of day you've had.

- Call your manager and talk things over with her or him.

- Become involved in company activities which take place outside of normal business situations; the golf outing, the annual dinner dance etc.

- Make sure that everyone in your organisation knows that you are part of the organisation too!

Geographically, some of these ideas may be more difficult for some of you than for others, but if you feel isolated you have to make the effort.

ORGANISATION AND PERSONAL DISCIPLINE

For most of us working from home, *organisation* and *personal discipline* are our biggest problems, so I have put together a few pointers – dare I say rules – to help you in this situation:

1 Don't work off of the kitchen table. With the best will in the world it will always feel like the kitchen table!
2 Create your own little office at home, you don't need a separate study – although if you have one that's great.
3 Buy yourself a writing bureau and a small filing cabinet. Make your workspace feel like an office – it won't cost a lot

of money and it will make a significant difference to your professional attitude.

4 Make sure that you have all the relevant files, information etc., that you would have if you were working from your office. You will usually find that space is at a premium at home so whenever you find that you have accumulated some out of date literature, price lists etc., send them back to the office or throw them out – you won't use them again anyway.

5 If you find yourself at home in the morning, because you are making telephone calls or preparing some kind of report or proposal etc., get out of bed at the normal time, shower, dress as if for the office and be ready to begin work at your normal time.

6 Don't lounge around in your dressing gown, or take the children to school or drop your husband, or wife, off at the railway station – you're at your work – behave as if you are.

7 If you wouldn't wear your carpet slippers to the office, don't wear them when you're working from home – wear your shoes.

8 Turn the television and the radio off – unless of course they are normally on in your office.

9 Discourage telephone calls, during your working time at home, which come from your boyfriend/girlfriend, husband/wife, family, friends etc. They wouldn't call you every ten minutes at the office – so don't let them do so when you're working from your 'home office'.

The ability to work successfully from home is all about creating the right frame of mind. If you treat the situation such that you feel as if you are at home, you will never get any work done.

125

In my own personal situation I work predominantly from home, where I at least have the advantage of having a separate study complete with computer, printer, fax, telephone, filing cabinets – the lot. Yet, every time I am at home, people call me up and say things like, 'Aren't you working today?'

I have taken to getting up in the morning and removing my car from the driveway – hiding the damn thing a couple of streets away from where I live – just so that friends who are passing don't drop in to see me.

SUMMARY

- Your mobile office should only have the materials you will need for today. Don't make it appear that you have left home permanently.

- Get to know the real people who are your customers and keep private record cards with the necessary information.

- Create a flexible diary system which suits you and your business.

- If you intend to use a computerised diary system, make sure that you understand it and that you can make good use of it.

- If you don't have a mobile or portable telephone it's not the end of the world! If you do have one, make sure that it's used to best advantage and isn't just another 'toy'.

- Understand that working from home is different from working from an office and that you could begin to feel isolated. Don't let it happen.

- Organise yourself such that it feels like you're working from an office.

6

Some special situations

In this chapter, I would like to address some of the **special situations** in which you will find yourself, often without any real training in how to handle most of them. Before we do that, however, perhaps it would be a good idea to make sure that we first put some of the basics in place. I deliberately include in these a subject that I consider to be one of the basics but which is introduced here because of its conspicuous absence in day to day selling.

Pre-call planning

A fair amount of 'lip service' is paid to planning before going into the call, but my experience suggests that in the majority of cases, sales people – and indeed their managers – tend to make it up in the call as they go along. I refer to it as 'busking'; because it's the type of impromptu performance that you're likely to see from a street entertainer.

If you don't prepare in depth before you go into the call, don't be surprised if you come back out as empty-handed as you went in!

Three questions you will need to ask yourself before going into any call are:

- What is the *main objective* of the call?

- To what do I need to win their agreement in order to build towards securing that main objective? I refer to these as *stages of agreement*.

- In the event that I don't secure my main objective in this call, what will be the different *fall back positions* I can adopt?

Figure 6.1 will help you prepare for future sales calls.

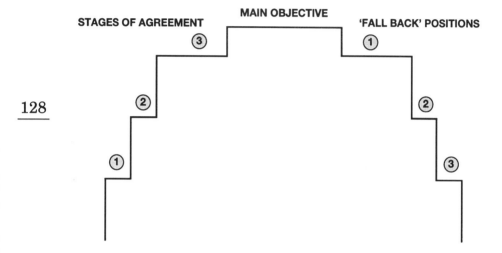

Fig. 6.1 The Pre-call Planning Document

Don't rely on memory in these situations, write one of these out for each call – immediately before you go in, in case you forget in the heat of the moment.

Most sales people with whom I have worked have a main objective in mind before they go into a meeting with a customer or prospect. Surprisingly that main objective isn't always as clear as it might be.

By that I mean that their objective may be to 'get an order'. A clearly defined objective would be the exact type of order they hope to win.

Very few have a really clear cut idea of the stages they need to go through and the agreement they need to reach with the customer in order to build towards securing the main objective. Even fewer have any idea at all of what they should do in the event that they don't secure the main objective, albeit only at this meeting. When that situation arises, the majority of them literally panic and leave the meeting having secured nothing concrete, not even a return appointment.

Allow me to expand a little to improve your understanding of the entire process.

When I am conducting training programmes, many people insist that they go into meetings where the main objective is to get information from the customer or prospect. That would only ever be a *stage* in the process! The real main objective would be the commitment from the customer to the next course of action based on that information.

129

That situation applies in my business, where I need the information to be able to put together a programme outline of what training I would conduct, for whom, what the objectives would be, how long it would take and what the fees would be, based on all of that.

The real main objective would be that I get commitment to a return appointment at which I would be able to make a presentation together with recommendations for action. Furthermore, if my presentation is found to be acceptable there would be commitment to doing business. For most of you, however, your main objective will be to make a specific sale.

One of the stages you will go through will be to get the information and gain the customer's agreement to the fact that this is the real situation, so that you can make your presentation – there and then – based on that information!

For those of you who have to work on a multiple-call sale, you may initially think that *information gathering* could be a main objective for the first of these calls. That main objective is not sufficiently clearly defined to enable you to achieve all that you can in that call.

As one of your stages, but only ever a stage, you will need the information to identify a need or a desire on the customer's part for the type of product or service that you are selling. Another stage would be the customer's agreement that these needs and desires had been correctly identified. The real objective of the call would be to secure the customer's agreement that, having correctly identified the needs and desires, you would be able to return with your recommendations or proposals based on those agreed needs – and indeed if those recommendations or proposals are acceptable that the customer will commit to doing business with you.

I have been racking my brains, which my friends would assure you isn't a very long exercise, to think of any situation which I can recall where information gathering could be a main objective and quite simply I can't. Nevertheless, whatever the main objective might be, let us now take a look at some of your fall back positions.

If we return to the situation which is most common, that of winning an order in the call, what would these fall backs be if you didn't win the original order which was your main objective?

- Perhaps a smaller order, to be used as a trial?
- Perhaps agreement to the testing of some samples?

- Perhaps a meeting with some technical people to satisfy the customer that your product is up to the standard of specification required?

- Perhaps only the agreement to a further meeting to take your discussion to the next stage?

Whatever the fall back positions are, if you don't have them clear in your mind before you go into the meeting, you may forget and come out having achieved little or nothing.

I have been working recently with a group of sales people who are involved in a multiple-call sale. (There are quite a few businesses where this is the case, but I often wonder how many times sales people create a multiple-call sale where it isn't really necessary.) However, in working with these people, who genuinely do have a multiple-call sale situation, one of their major 'excuses' is that they are often only used as a price-checking service to satisfy the customer or prospect that their current supplier, with whom they are happy, is still delivering value for money.

My answer to that has to be that they become involved in these situations purely and simply because they didn't make the main objective of the call the agreement to doing business, if the recommendations at the follow-up meeting were found to be acceptable.

Post-call analysis

Two things happen when we come out of a call:

1 We have won an order and we're trying to get back to the car without showing too much delight to the customer.

2 We have failed to secure an order and as well as trying not to show too much disappointment, we're too shell-shocked to think what could have gone wrong.

The following diagram, which is an extension of the previous one, will help you analyse what went on in the call.

It isn't too uncommon for sales people to try to analyse what went wrong in sales calls, but it is extremely rare for them to take the time out to analyse what went right – particularly if an order was won. So use Figure 6.2 to look at what happened regarding your *stages*, your *main objective* and your *fall back positions*, as well as thinking about the *objections* you met and how you handled them – or failed to handle them.

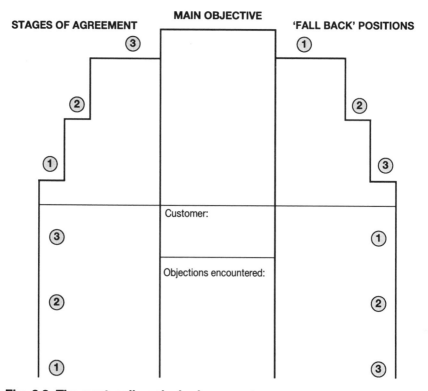

Fig. 6.2 The post-call analysis document

While all of the things that I have written in this section apply to normal 'one-to-one' selling situations, the need for the main objectives, stages of agreement and fall back positions becomes even more important when selling to *groups*.

Selling to groups

There is a growing tendency among customers to involve groups of people in the decision-making process, with the result that you will often find when you arrange appointments that you are confronted with more than one person.

My personal belief is that this has less to do with meaningful input from the extra people who have been drafted into the meeting than it has with being able to share the responsibility if the decision turns out to be less favourable than expected. The classic, 'It wasn't me and I wasn't the only one!' excuse.

133

There is also the situation where the customer or prospect has involved a 'group' of people as a tactic for the meeting. **Note:** My definition of a group is more than one person. However, those things aside, the simple fact of life is that you will more frequently find yourselves 'outnumbered' when you sit down face to face with customers and prospects.

There are basically three types of situation where you will find yourselves having to sell to groups of people:

1 The one where the situation appears to be straightforward, but you find when you arrive that there is more than one person involved.
2 The situation where the nature and perhaps the value of the business being discussed is such that you would expect

that there would be input from 'specialists' at such a meeting.

3 A major or *key account* situation where not only does the customer have a group of people present, so do you.

BEFORE THE GROUP CALL

In the first situation which I have described above, there may not be the opportunity to carry out any type of in depth pre-call planning, but if there is, some of the following should be considered:

- How many people will be there?
- Who are they?
- What are their respective positions?
- Who are the more senior in the organisation?
- Why are they there?
- Why do they think you are there?
- With whom was the meeting originally arranged?
- Will a decision be made at this meeting?

If it genuinely is the situation which I describe in (1) above, you may have to ask some of those questions in the meeting. **Remember**, don't be afraid to ask, don't leave yourself groping around in the dark and don't be intimidated. Think about it; if the customer has had to pull in a group of people to share the decision responsibility, or as a tactic, the chances are that they're more afraid of you than you should be of them!

If the situation falls into that described in (2) above, then you should be asking all of these questions of your original contact – before you arrive at the meeting.

I recall some years ago becoming involved in a situation which fell into number (1) above.

I had been approached by the managing director of Terex Equipment in Scotland, which at that time was the earth moving equipment division of General Motors. The full story behind this is told in *The Ultimate USP is You*, but basically the approach came about as a result of a poor third-party reference being used by one of my competitors.

It transpired that the personnel manager had sent me a letter outlining who would be present at this meeting, but the letter didn't arrive at my office until two days after the meeting. I arrived for what I thought was an initial meeting with the managing director, to find that I was taken to the *training suite* which Terex had on site and that the Board of Directors was present, with the exception of the assistant managing director, together with most of the Heads of the various departments, in total a group of some 12 people.

As it was the training suite, the room was laid out in a typical 'U' formation so I decided that it was time that I took control of the situation before it ran away from me. I took my chair and placed it in the middle of the 'U' such that I could see everyone and they could talk to me – similar to an interview panel situation. The one thing they now thought was that I wasn't afraid of or intimidated by them. **Little did they know!**

My next move was to delve into my briefcase and extract some blank sheets of A4 paper and some flip chart felt-tipped markers which I handed out with the request that they all write their names – including first names – and their positions on the paper and fold them in front of them in such a way that it created 'name cards'. My explanation was quite simply that with a group of that size it would be difficult for me to remember all of their names, and that I hadn't received the letter that the Personnel Manager had sent me prior to the meeting.

While they were doing this, I asked the personnel manager for permission to set up the overhead projector. This having been done, I took from my briefcase some preprepared overhead projector acetates which I carry for presentation purposes and was now as ready as I was ever going to be.

I should say to you at this point, that having felt-tipped markers and acetates etc., is part and parcel of my business, so I wouldn't expect all of you to find yourselves so conveniently prepared – but perhaps you should think about it.

As I looked around the room I could now see who were directors, who were managers and what their various areas of responsibility were.

My first question to them was simple but appeared to elicit some surprise; 'Gentlemen, why do you think I am here?'

The sales director, Bob Wallace, answered on behalf of the group and said, 'We have already had a presentation on training from X Y Z Consultants (it would be unprofessional to name them), and we have come here so that you can also make a presentation to us'. I replied by outlining the circumstances which had led up to my presence, including the telephone call from the managing director. I then quietly placed an acetate on the overhead projector which read:

> **'You can't propose a solution until you understand the problem!'**

I spent the next hour asking them all of the questions which I gave you earlier in this section – and quite a few more. At the end, they agreed to delegate four of the directors and managers – each to arrange half-day meetings with me so that I could understand the problems and make a proper professional presentation with regard to my recommended solutions. Earlier in this book I reminded you that the real decision makers are busy people – so I was delighted to have that degree of commitment from this group, even before I made any presentation.

AT THE GROUP CALL

137

A question you will want to ask of yourself *before* you go into any of these group meetings will be, 'Having carried out as much precall planning as possible, how will I then handle the situation while in the meeting with that group of people?'

The first thing to arrange is the seating.

This is not as difficult as you may think, you only need to give the group a reason for the way that the seating should be organised. If you intend to make some type of formal presentation using visual aids, perhaps also a flip chart or an overhead projector, you would want to position yourself in much the same way that I described in my Terex meeting, where everyone can see you and your presentation and where you can see all of them. That being the case, if you don't want to hand out 'name cards', you will need to make a quick sketch on a piece of paper so that you know who is seated where.

If you don't intend to make a formal presentation, or if this is the first call in a multiple call situation, make sure that you seat yourself within the group. Don't allow a 'you versus them' situation to develop, where you are at one side of the table and they are all at the other. The sooner you create the psychological perception that you are all working together to arrive at agreement the better it will work for you.

It is becoming more common in customers' offices for there to be some sort of informal 'coffee table' type set up to be used. If the group is large enough, the meeting will usually be held in a separate meeting room. Both of these situations make it easier to become a part of the group.

Remember, you must take control of the situation or by sheer weight of numbers the meeting will run away from you. Begin to ask your questions and listen carefully. The people in the meeting who are really responsible will make themselves known to you either by the fact that they are doing most of the talking or by the type of answers they give to your questions.

If you don't know who everybody is, ask! Also ask about their respective positions. Ask what their specific interest is in the meeting. Ask why they think you are there. And, finally, ask if a decision will be made at this meeting.

During the course of the meeting a number of different characters will appear:

- *Those who are for* you and/or your 'project'.

- *Those who are against* you and/or your 'project'.

- *Those who are sitting on the fence*, waiting to gauge the reaction of another member of the meeting.

- *Those who remain quiet*, perhaps because they have a 'hidden agenda' – maybe they have an otherwise vested interest.

So, how should you handle each of these?

A lot will depend on the seniority of the members of the group who adopt the different attitudes. The *fence sitters* will usually not be the more senior in the group, so you will need to identify whose opinion it is that they are waiting to gauge. The ones who *remain quiet* will need to be drawn into the conversation, otherwise you will never discover if there is a hidden agenda, or if they are simply disinterested and have been 'press ganged' into the meeting.

With *those who are against*, you will need to discover why – and the effect that a decision in your favour would have on them. With *those who are for*, you will need to identify the amount of power they hold within the group and even if they have most power, how much their opinion will be swayed by the other members – and who these other members are. Address your conversation, in the main, to the ones who are for you. If they have sufficient power they will usually carry those who are against with them. However, beware that you don't ignore anyone – even the fence sitters.

139

Earlier in this book I used the acronym the MAN as a way of identifying the decision makers. In *The Ultimate USP is You* I also refer to the AID, i.e. the people who have the **Ability to Influence the Decision**. If it isn't entirely clear in your meeting who these are, the following may help you to identify them by the questions they ask or their responses to your questions or suggestions.

Some of the things in which the MAN will be interested are:

- Does it do the job?

- What return can be expected on the investment?

- Is it needed?

- Conversely, can it be done without?

- Is there a budget available to buy it?

- How will the purchase affect the cash flow of the company?

- Is it in keeping with the company's image?

- How would the purchase be affected by company policy?

Some of the things in which the AID will be interested are:

- How does it work?

- How will it affect her or him?

- Is it reliable?

- Is it safe?

- Is it efficient?

- Is it simple to use?

- Is it easy to maintain?

Obviously these areas of interest will change according to what it is you are selling, e.g. if you were selling advertising, maintenance and simplicity of use would not come into consideration, but the clues are in the different areas of interest to enable you to apply this thinking to your own personal situations.

Whenever you have identified the people who would qualify as the MAN and those who would come under the description of the AID, be careful not to come down too obviously in favour of the AIDs against the MAN for fear that the real decision maker feels that he or she is being backed into a corner.

THE TACTICS BETWEEN MEETINGS

In a multiple-call situation, assuming that you have at least won the commitment of the group to a follow-up meeting and presentation, what can you do between the first meeting and the follow up?

The answer is you 'lobby'.

During your first meeting you will have established some rapport with at least one member of your customer's or prospect's group – often your original contact, who after all put her or his head on the block to arrange the meeting in the first place. There may also be others. You need to generate a situation where you can talk to these people before you return for your formal presentation.

I try to leave a meeting, such as I've described, with the agreement that should I need further information prior to my return appointment then I will be able to call on one or two of the members of the group to acquire that information or clarify my understanding. This is the time when I usually get back to the people with whom I have established some rapport and, in a 'one to one' situation, ask some of the questions which may have been inappropriate in the larger group, such as:

- Who holds the real power?
- Who will be affected adversely or favourably by the decision?
- Who is for me and who is against me?

I've even been known to seek advice on how to handle some of these people and the situations.

It usually works – try it!

If I refer you back to the Terex equipment situation, that is exactly what I did. I kept my pre-arranged meetings with the directors and managers with whom these had been agreed. I also had meetings with the people whom I felt were for me and the project and with whom I had established rapport.

During these meetings, I was able to establish who was for and who was against the project and why. I also established the 'fence sitters' and on whose side they were likely to come down. I found out who would be most affected by the decision to carry out the training and interestingly was able to discover why the assistant managing director had been absent from the initial meeting – and that he would definitely be present at the follow-up meeting. With this information I was able to work out my strategy for the presentation meeting.

MAKING THE PRESENTATION

If the geography makes it possible and the project is sufficiently valuable to you and the customer, try to arrange the presentation meeting in your company's premises. This means that you can organise the layout of the room, you can have a manager or director of your company join the meeting and psychologically, you are already ahead because you are on *your* territory and not the customer's.

However, whether the meeting takes place in your premises or the customer's, the following will apply:

1 When you have established who will attend your presentation meeting, take copies of your proposals for everyone present.
2 If you can arrange it, make name cards for each – so that you can arrange the seating.
3 Arrive half an hour before the meeting in order to 'set

things up'; room layout, flip chart, overhead projector, presentation material etc.

4 Use your main contact in the company to allow you access to the meeting room for this purpose.

5 Arrange for coffee and tea to be served a few minutes before the end of your presentation. If this is in your customer's premises, I would be surprised if you weren't able to organise this through your main contact.

6 During your presentation, make good use of the information you were able to acquire during the 'lobbying' of your contacts.

7 Using the other points that I have given you, ensure that you remain in control of the meeting.

8 Make sure that you get impact early and don't be afraid of being provocative.

143

Let me provide you with an example by completing my Terex story for you. You may recall that I told you that the original meeting came about because of the bad use of a third-party reference by one of my competitors which had resulted in the Terex managing director calling me. I opened my presentation meeting with the following statement:

> 'Gentlemen, I shouldn't be here. The reason why I am here is that X Y Z Consultants want to teach *your people how to sell.* In the process of trying to prove to you that they are capable of doing this, they gave your managing director *another company's name a*s a reference, which when taken up by him resulted in *his* being referred to *me'.*

Don't throw away an opportunity to get some real impact, particularly if this can be done to emphasise one of your strengths and exploit a competitor's weaknesses.

Before I leave the subject of selling to groups, let me refer back to the third situation which I outlined earlier, the one where both your company and the customer have a group of people present. There are some basic guidelines which you will want to follow to make best use of these situations.

In the initial meeting you will need to agree with your colleagues who will do most of the talking and who will handle questions in the different areas of the discussion. For example, there would be little point in taking your company's technical manager into the meeting if his or her remit was not to handle the technical aspects of the discussion. However, make sure that he or she sticks to that remit and doesn't try to take over the selling side of the meeting. I know it can be difficult to shut them up once they get started, but don't allow non-sales people to take over the discussion.

The easiest and most polite way of interrupting someone is to use his or her name. Do it in such a way that you don't convey any annoyance to either your colleague or your customer, e.g. 'Kate, (pause to allow the person to stop talking) I'm sorry to interrupt, but while you were speaking something occurred to me that may be relevant . . .' Then gently steer the conversation back to the point. If you use this method of interruption, you can also do it with a customer whose conversation has strayed from the point of the discussion.

In the presentation meeting, make sure that everyone on your team has rehearsed exactly what they are going to do. Know who will effectively 'chair' the meeting, who will make the introduction and who will make the different parts of the presentation, and why. When there is a handover between the different members of your team, make it smooth and professional and don't leave this part of the presentation hanging in the air. Make it as professional as you possibly can. Your customer or prospect will be as impressed by the professionalism of the presentation as they will be by the content.

HOW TO GET THE DECISION

Make it implicit within your presentation that you expect a decision at this meeting. When the coffee and tea is served and you have answered any questions put to you as a result of your presentation, offer to leave the room for ten minutes, or however long the group needs, in order that they may speak freely and arrive at their decision. You will find that there are occasions when the group will be unwilling to offer their decision there and then. But if you don't ask, they are extremely unlikely to offer.

145

If the customer can't or won't give a decision at the meeting, you need to agree a timetable for the decision. Based on this timetable try to set up an appointment on a 'one-to-one' basis with whoever has been delegated to relay the decision to you. You may get the offer of a telephone call, but my experience has been that, if the decision goes against you, the call will not materialise, you will receive instead the infamous 'thanks but no thanks' letter. Only when it is in your favour will the telephone call be made.

Let's take some time now to look at another *special situation* in which you will often find yourself.

Selling with your manager round your neck

For most of us this is an extremely stressful situation. Why?

There are a number of reasons, including some of the following:

- The manager hasn't made it clear why he or she is there.
- We think that he or she is adopting a 'police-like' role.
- We know from previous experience that the manager will take over the situation.
- We also know from previous experience that the manager will not only take over, he or she will make a complete mess of the situation!
- We haven't planned the day as well as we might – and there may even have been an element of creativity in the forward call plan submitted to him or her. In short, we may not have some of the confirmed appointments that we said we had.

You'll know when the manager is acting in a police role – you will arrive at the call to find him or her waiting for you with no prearrangement having been made between you.

If your fear and trepidation is due to a 'creative' call plan – own up and don't let it happen again.

So, if we set these two aside, let us look at the best way to conduct these accompanied calls.

You need to work with your manager to plan in advance the following:

- The purpose of the accompaniment.
- Discussions between you *before* each call.
- The role of each of you during the call.
- Discussions between you *after* each call.

WHAT IS THE PURPOSE OF THE ACCOMPANIMENT?

It could be:

- For the manager to get information straight from the field.

- For the manager to give you information.

- For the manager to check that previous decisions made between you are being carried out.

- For the manager to educate, train and develop you 'on the job'.

- For the manager to handle a delicate situation with a customer as a result of you being backed into a corner.

- For the manager to give you moral support in a tricky situation.

WHAT SHOULD YOU DISCUSS BEFORE EACH CALL?

- The main objectives of the call.

- The stages of agreement that you need.

- The fall back positions that you have.

- What you know about the customer.

- Any further information that you need.

- The various selling aids that you will use.

- How you will co-operate in the call.

- Who will do the talking – and why.

- How you introduce the manager in the call.

You will have prepared the main objectives, the stages of agreement and the fall backs using the form I gave you earlier – **won't you?** Get your manager to go over these with you, he or she may have some suggestions for improvement.

It's usually good to have somebody else's thoughts on the matter.

Discuss what you already know about this customer. Your manager may know more from previous experience and be able to supplement this information. Agree between you what additional information you need to enhance your ability to conclude the sale, and agree the best selling aids to use – and how you will use them.

With the exception of the call where the manager has come in to 'get you back out of a corner', agree that **YOU** will do **ALL** the talking! Also agree on a method of ensuring that the manager will continually hand the conversation back to you if the customer tries to get the manager to conduct the call.

Decide whether the manager will be introduced as such or whether he or she will be introduced as a colleague, and decide on an explanation for her or his presence. Customers can become ill at ease if they think that they're being put under pressure.

For years I have advocated that the manager should be introduced as a colleague, for the reason that the customer will always want to talk to the manager, thinking that a better offer is available. Their attitude is one of preferring to talk to the organ grinder rather than the monkey!

The occasions when I have had resistance to this idea have invariably come from managers who, when they accompany their sales people, embark on a demented ego trip! This is when they take over the call and, even if they don't make a complete mess of it, they erode the sales person's credibility with their customer.

There are situations, however, when I do advocate that the

manager is introduced as such. These could be:

- When the customer knows the manager.
- When it is important to the situation that the manager is present.
- When it's patently obvious to the customer that the manager is senior to you in your company.

I had a situation recently which developed along similar lines to my last statement. I was conducting some field research before carrying out a training programme and was making a number of calls with sales people in order that I understood the business before finalising the design of the programme.

I went into a call with one of the sales people, who merely introduced me by name and made no explanation for my presence. It soon became obvious that the customer wanted to carry on the conversation with me, about a range of products which, at that time, I would have had difficulty in identifying had I found them floating in my soup!

149

It was obvious that the customer thought that I was someone senior in the company. I had to explain, because the sales person hadn't, who I was and why I was there. The interesting thing was that the customer was so impressed that my client company – his supplier – was prepared to invest time and money in improving the performance of its sales force, that he perceived it in terms of it leading to an improved quality of service for his own company.

WHAT DO EACH OF YOU DO IN THE CALL?

As I said before, *you* will do all the talking. The exception to this is when you really lose control of the situation, then your manager should intervene – careful of your image with the customer – to get the situation back on track. As soon as this has been done, he or she should hand the call back over to you. At the end of the day, however, the business comes first, so if you have lost control, the manager should conclude the sale and explain to you after the call what happened and why, and what you can do about it in future.

Your job in the call is to be as relaxed and natural as you would if you were on your own so that the manager gets a real idea of the quality of your selling skills.

The manager's job in the call is to observe what happened, assist you to maintain control of the call and be in a position afterwards to offer some advice or guidance for future calls.

WHAT DO YOU DO AFTER THE CALL?

Together you will analyse what happened in the call:

- Did you achieve your main objective?
- Did you secure the various stages of agreement along the way?
- What fall back positions did you have to adopt?
- What commitment did you secure to the next stage?
- What will you do about preparing for the next stage?
- What objections came up – and how well did you handle them?

The manager will give you an honest evaluation of the level of selling skills exhibited in the call and, where necessary, some suggestions for improvement.

What I've outlined above is classically referred to as *The Kerbside Conference*, except these days it's usually conducted in the car. I would suggest that you drive away from the customer's premises before you carry this out and park in some quiet place where the analysis can be carried out. If you carry this out at the customer's premises, and your contact there observes your discussion, he or she may think that you are having some sort of disagreement. Worse, he or she may get the impression that you are involved in a discussion relating to your offer and may think, wrongly, that there is an improvement available.

At the end of the day with your manager, you should both sit down somewhere quietly, maybe over a cup of coffee, and analyse the whole day, the quality of the calls, the successes and failures and agree on what action you will jointly take as a result.

151

It may be that some additional coaching is needed. It may be that based on the skills you have exhibited, you could be used in a coaching rôle with some of your colleagues. What-ever it is, you need to have some concrete action coming as a result of the day, or you could end up feeling that the manag-er's real reason for accompanying you is that there wasn't anything better to do.

SUMMARY

- When selling to anyone the need for *precall planning* is really important.

- *Identify* your *main objectives*, the *stages of agreement* and your *fall back positions.*

- Make sure that your *main objectives* are clearly defined.

- When selling to *groups* the need for *precall planning* is critical.

- Recognise who is *for*, who is *against* and who is *sitting on the fence* – and why.

- Identify the *MAN* and the *AID* (the *decision makers* and the *influencers*).

- In multiple call situations, become involved in *'lobbying'* activities between the calls.

- *Rehearse your presentation* – particularly with regard to getting the decision.

- *Maintain control* of the meeting.

- When you are accompanied by your manager on calls, *agree the reasons* for the accompaniment.

- *Discuss the arrangements* before each call.

- Agree on your *strategy* in the call.

- Conduct an *open and honest analysis* after each call and after the day.

- Don't be *afraid* of being accompanied – use these times as *opportunities* for you to develop as a sales person.

7

Let's talk about negotiating

Responsibility without authority

Dr Vernon Coleman in his work, '*Stress Management Techniques*', says '**N**ever give **A**uthority without **R**esponsibility and **N**ever give **R**esponsibility without **A**uthority'.

The problem is that as sales people this will happen to you on a daily basis. In other words, you will be given the *responsibility* to 'negotiate' business with your customers but you won't be given the *authority* to make decisions. I call it 'having to get the results with one hand tied behind your back'.

One of the real problems is in the use of the word 'negotiate'. Very few sales people are genuinely put in the position where they can 'negotiate'. The word has become devalued by people who either don't like the word 'sell' or think that negotiating is an up-market expression for selling.

I frequently come across people who would like to participate in a *negotiating skills* programme when what they really need is a *selling skills* programme. Too many think that they are one and the same thing, when in fact you can't begin to negotiate until you have learned to sell.

However, I can relate to sales managers and directors who don't allow sales people the authority to make decisions relative to price etc., purely and simply because of the amount of abuse that I have seen sales people give such authority.

You only need to walk into a motor car showroom during times when car sales are low to discover that the average sales person's *opening gambit* is a percentage discount higher than you had thought you could negotiate after some ferocious haggling. Obviously if that is the starting point, you know you can get more.

I worked with an office-equipment company some years ago which allowed its sales people to give discounts of up to 25 per cent, without referring back to the management. The number of sales people who took the line of least resistance and gave away discounts with little or no commitment in return from the customer was appalling. As if that wasn't bad enough, by opening with high discounts many of them ended up having to go back to the management because they had been backed into a corner. I also noted that to justify these situations there was a great deal of creativity in the stories that were used regarding future business from these customers, which, 'surprise, surprise', never seemed to materialise at the end of the day.

NEGOTIATING FROM A POSITION OF WEAKNESS

However, in order to untie that hand from behind your back, I would like to make some suggestions regarding the various things that sales people should be allowed to negotiate, and if you want the authority to go with the responsibility, ask your manager or director to consider some of these possible variables:

- Price.
- Retrospective discounts.
- Early settlement discounts.
- Extended payment terms.

- 'Call off' orders.
- Collection instead of delivery.
- Just in Time supply.

These are the most common, but there may be others in your business, such as 'free' samples, trial packs etc. Discuss these with your manager.

In the meantime, let us explore the list that I have created:

1 **Price** – or more appropriately discounts on the list price. This is a particularly good area in which sales people could be given authority to negotiate, but not in the way that I described in my reference to the motor car showroom situation. Get your company to give you discount bands on the basis of volume of business, tonnes etc., or on financial order value.

This creates the situation that I have always favoured, which is that you can offer the customer a better price, providing he or she offers you a better order.

2 **Retrospective discounts.**
Another good area for sales people. Devise a banding system whereby the customer will be given a retrospective discount on the basis of the total amount of business done over a given period, usually a year.

My experience has been that as the end of the period draws near, the customer begins to look seriously at the amount of business done and, where this comes close to the next higher discount band, the volume of business is increased to take advantage of this. This is particularly true of situations where the customer is involved in multiple sourcing, e.g. consumables such as photocopier paper, printer ribbons or cassettes, PC floppy disks etc.

155

3 Early settlement discounts.

Many of you will be working with companies who have to keep a tight control over their cash flow. In such situations, offer a discount if the customer is prepared and in a position to settle your invoices earlier than your normal terms of business.

I know of one Brewery chain in the UK who, as a matter of purchasing policy, automatically requests a discount for early settlement. This policy is based on the fact that the majority of their business is in a positive cash flow position. In my own business I have used all of the above when negotiating with clients, with the proviso on the early settlement discount that if the discount is deducted by the client but the invoice isn't settled within the agreed time, I submit a further invoice for the difference.

The alternative to early settlement discounts is:

4 Extended payment terms.

If you work for a large organisation where cash flow is relatively unimportant, perhaps you should consider offering an extension to your payment terms. If your customers are small businesses where cash flow is vital to them, you may be able to secure the business at good prices for your company by extending your normal payment terms from say 30 days to 45 days.

You would have to make sure that the customer was credit worthy and that there was no real risk attached to your offer, but if you think about it, most of them take 45 days anyway. Why not consider making it official and using it as a lever to secure the additional business?

5 'Call off' orders.

This is another tactic I have personally used in my own business, but in this case as a customer. The company that manufactures the special A4 ring binders that I use on training programmes need a minimum order quantity. I give them an order for a year's supply of these binders, but call them off in quantities of 50 at a time, paying for them on the basis of the 'call off'. My problem isn't the ability to pay for the total order, it's the ability to store it!

I negotiate a further discount from them by collecting the binders instead of them being delivered and for settling the bill on collection. I have a client who is one of the largest multinationals in the world, with a great deal of purchasing power, who hasn't managed to buy these binders at anything close to my price – simply because they haven't negotiated the deal.

157

6 Collection instead of delivery.

As I mentioned above, if your product and the location of your business lends itself to it, consider offering the customer a better price for collecting the goods instead of having them delivered. Even if you charge for delivery, think of the cost of administering that service. It's also another edge you can have when negotiating the contract.

7 Just in Time supply.

This is similar to the 'call off' situation I described before, except that the orders aren't called off, they are supplied to a predetermined schedule.

Negotiate a contract with your customer for a 'bulk' order and agree at the same time a schedule of deliveries, perhaps once a week or month, and ship the goods out based on that schedule.

The drive among companies these days for Just in Time management is such that this offer should have more than its fair share of appeal. The only potential problem is that you need to make sure that your own company is capable of meeting the schedule.

With all of the variables that I have outlined here, the main point should be that if you are given the authority to negotiate on any or all of these, there should be clearly defined criteria laid down by your management to help you make the decisions.

If you have managed to get your manager or director to give you the necessary authority, here are some guidelines that will help you in genuine negotiations.

Negotiating with authority

There have been a great many books written on this subject and I don't propose here to try to cover all that is in these books.

What I would like to do is give you some key points which will help you along the way. Remember, customers need to buy our products and services as much as we need to sell them. What we need to do is identify the reasons why the customer will buy from us and not our competitors. This is where negotiation can help.

Although we may have established a number of variables around which we can negotiate, the most common area by far will be that of price. So let's revisit price discounts of all types.

Some of the things that you **should do** include:

1 Be creative with your discounting.
2 Use discounts to clear stocks.
3 Offer discounts for *extra* business.

4 If you're selling through an intermediary – someone who sells your product on to the end user – try to make sure that the discounts are passed on to the end user. In that way your company will increase its share of the overall market.

5 Use different discount structures for different product groups.

6 If you offer a discount for early settlement and they take the discount, but don't settle within the agreed time, send them another bill for the discount!

7 If you offer a special discount – put a time limit on it to prevent them using you as a lever in an 'auction' between you and the competition.

Some of the things that you **should not do**:

159

1 Offer discounts simply because everybody else does – try to sell the benefits of your product or service first.

2 Discount where there is no need to.

3 Publish discount tables as if they were for all time.

4 Send them in the mail-like brochures – the competition will get their hands on them.

5 Give away discounts with new or unique products. In times when business is good, try to get a discount on a Mercedes-Benz, *I dare you*!

6 Leave the offer of discounts to your manager, it erodes your credibility.

The real problems with discounting, particularly if it's simply a 'give away' is establishing how much to give and determining if they will find out from another customer that you gave them more.

John Winkler in his book *'Pricing for Results'*, has some nice thoughts in this respect; 'The extra profit you chisel on the first deal could cost you a fortune in later ones'. He also says, 'Buyers can be real miseries when they try hard, their mothers should have kissed them more'.

From the same book is probably one of the best pieces of advice I have ever read, 'Practise saying "NO!" – you can always change your mind and say "YES" later. What's all the hurry?'

While we are on the subject of discounting and price, let's look at some **price negotiating strategies**:

1 Try to get the customer to make the opening gambit.
2 Avoid conflict and don't confuse assertiveness with aggression. You might win the argument but you'll certainly lose the sale!
3 Don't be indecisive, the customer will see this as weakness and try to put pressure on you – often successfully.
4 Be firm and confident and convince the customer that you can deliver what you promise.
5 As well as identifying that the customer needs what you offer – get the customer to *want* it, *from you*!
6 Decide what you want before you go into the meeting and test the feasibility of success with good open questions.
7 Know what your bottom line is and be prepared to leave if the customer's demands are too high.

In number six above I refer to good open questions. Those of you who read *The Ultimate USP is You* will have a greater insight into these as well as using 'digging for gold', the technique for controlling the conversation. If, however, you haven't yet done so, let me give you some pointers for questioning in the negotiation:

- *Use open questions.* These are readily identified by the fact that they begin with one of the following words: **who, why, what, where, when, how, which.**

- *Listen to the answers.* Most sales people think that you need the ability to talk to make you successful. You do, but more importantly you need the ability to *listen!*

- *Hear the customer out.* Don't interrupt; as well as being rude, it also breaks the flow of the conversation.

- *Don't ask too many questions.* The customer wants to feel that this is a conversation – not an interrogation.

- *Be careful with weakening questions.* Questions which directly appear to weaken the customer's position will create a negative effect and those which appear to weaken your position will be used against you later in the negotiation.

- *Watch for defensiveness.* If the customer becomes defensive you will have to find out why? If you become defensive the customer may not want to discover why, but will certainly take advantage at a later stage.

161

- *Use surprise questions.* If you listen carefully you will be able to ask searching questions which will take the customer by surprise and make her or him sit up. These questions can often sway the customer in your direction, particularly if they convey the fact that you are taking a slightly different approach to the business than the rest of your competition.

- *Use checking questions.* Make sure that you have double-checked the possibilities, like the DMP etc. Think about the following points:

1 Who else will be involved in the decision?
2 What other factors need to be considered?
3 What else is involved?
4 Have we covered all of the criteria for making the decision?
5 Is there anything else?

Don't forget, however, that like selling there are distinct *rules* associated with the negotiating 'game':

■ Both you and the customer must care about each other's objectives. Remember I told you that to be in the negotiating game, the customer must need to buy as much as you need to sell.

■ Both of you must feel that the other was *fair* in the way that you conducted the negotiations.

■ Both of you must feel happy about doing business with each other in the future.

■ You must both be happy that the other will uphold whatever was agreed.

■ Everybody involved in the negotiation must feel that they have won!

It's often referred to as The 'Win–Win' philosophy.

Some time ago I was involved in the negotiation of a particular project with one of the divisions of a major client where The 'Win–Win' philosophy did not prevail. I had a meeting with the manager responsible for the project together with the director of the group company who had set up the meeting. At this meeting we agreed the nature, size and time scale of the project and, in my opinion – and that of the group director – we had agreed *fees* and *settlement terms*.

Shortly after this meeting I received a fax – not a telephone call – submitting an alternative proposal, which was considerably less than the original. My response to that was to send a return fax thanking the manager for his interest in the project and wishing him well in the future.

Within three hours I received a telephone call from the group director who had been called by the manager. The gist of their conversation was that the manager told the director about his fax to me and said that I had sent a return fax which suggested that I was no longer interested in the project.

The director actually said to the manager, 'Did the return fax contain any more than two words?' The manager responded by giving him the content of the fax and adding, 'Isn't Jim Cowden interested in the spirit of negotiation?'. Whereupon the director replied, 'As far as Jim Cowden is concerned you had already negotiated and agreed – and this is also my opinion. I would also like to suggest that if you want to start negotiating with him, you should nail your shirt to your back!'

163

The outcome was that the project did go ahead, but the manager obviously felt that he had lost and not won, so whenever invoices were due to be paid, they were always late – which was extremely unusual. Obviously the manager was paying me back in the only way that he could. It's a shame because the project was extremely successful, but the relationship had been soured.

To help you to manage your negotiations better and perhaps prevent you from falling into the type of 'trap' that I describe above, let me give you some **tactical hints** for when you're in a similar meeting:

- If the customer says something akin to 'I like it, but . . .', try to *clarify the situation* with the customer by asking *open questions* so that you discover the whole picture. Remember that everything before the BUT is bullshit! If someone is about to insult you they will say things like, 'I don't want to insult you, BUT . . .'. Whatever you hear before the BUT is untrue – in whole or in part.

- If the customer says, 'You've got to do better'. Don't fall for it. *Defend your position* and if necessary, *trade concessions* – so that you both give a little.

- If the customer tells you that he or she *hasn't the authority* to make the decision, it may be an excuse or a tactic. So find out the DMP as quickly as possible.

- If there are two people present from the customer's side and they're playing the 'hard man – soft man' routine, *keep calm* and *don't become flustered* – it's only a game!

Of course you will also come across the great '**poker faces**', the customers who once read that if they showed no emotion the sales person wouldn't be able to come to terms with the situation and consequently wouldn't be able to sell.

My personal experience is that the reason they show no emotion is that they have none. They are the obvious results of 'personality by-pass surgery' who have forgotten that they need to buy from someone. These are also the people who read about the strategic use of silence (a completely legitimate and powerful negotiating weapon), but also believed the idiot who told them that if they maintained silence, the first person to speak would be the loser.

Well, have we got news for them!

The way to handle these customers is to *keep asking open questions*, until they have to speak! First of all they will think – wrongly – that your questions are a sign of weakness and that they've won. Secondly, short of being absolutely rude, they will have to answer your questions. Finally, in so doing, they will be so wrapped up in their little game that they won't realise that they have given you the very information you need to be able to conclude a sale with them.

They will be resistant to it, but they *will* give in.

Then again, you will come across the type of customer who either begins the meeting with such *aggressive* questioning that you think you must have run over the office cat on your way into the call, or who *shows such anger* that you know they have graduated from the 'Attila the Hun' School of Management!

Remain calm and keep asking open questions – it will soon defuse the situation. It really is only with Attila the Hun that this tactic doesn't work!

Before we move on, let me give you a summary of the *stages of the negotiating process* of which there are four:

165

1 Preparation.

- Analyse what you have to offer.
- Analyse what the competition has to offer.
- Determine the parts of your offer that are of greatest value to the customer.
- Determine the variables of your offer which will cost you least to concede.
- Then decide upon your tactics.

2 Discussion.

- Use open questions to discover the customer's real situation.
- State your company's real situation.

3 Proposal.

- Explore all the possibilities thoroughly with the customer, testing the relative value of the variables.

4 Bargaining.

- Summarise the final agreement.

- Check that the customer's understanding of the agreement is the same as yours. (Don't fall into the same trap as I did in the situation I wrote about earlier in this chapter.)

- Shake hands on the agreement. Still one of the most powerful things you can do in business today!

- Confirm the agreement in writing.

Having given you some guidance on negotiating, I cannot stress too much, the most important rule of all; If you have the authority to use any or all of the variables mentioned, don't give them all away in the beginning or you will find yourself **being backed into a corner!**

I referred earlier to the office-equipment situation and people who found themselves backed into a corner, because their opening offer was too high, and the customer thought that more could be milked from the situation – usually quite correctly.

So what should you do if this happens to you?

1 Obviously prevention is better than cure and if you use some of the ideas outlined in this chapter and you have clear guidelines from your management team, you should be able to minimise the number of times that you find yourself in such a situation.

2 You could stand your ground and make it clear that there isn't anything more to be had. In this situation you run

the risk of 'deadlock' where the customer won't settle at your terms and you won't give any more so you lose the business.

What is more likely is that the customer will want to meet your manager or director, in the belief that someone senior to you will have the authority to give more. My observations in such situations are, regrettably, that when this happens the manager or director usually *does give more* – and your credibility with that customer has now gone. You may as well never call back again, other than to pick up a prearranged piece of business, because every time you get into a real selling situation the customer will never believe that what you say is your company's final offer.

167

3 You could tell your customer that you will need to refer back to your office. But if you have to, make it clear that they will expect a significantly better order in return! Of course, the customer may back off. But if they don't, make sure that when you return to the customer, you return alone. Otherwise you will create the situation of (2) above.

HOW TO GET BACK OUT OF THE CORNER

You will occasionally find yourself in situations where you still have more to give, if necessary, but need some breathing space to allow yourself to evaluate whether the business on offer is sufficient to warrant the extra. It may also be that you would like your customer to have time to consider whether their requests are reasonable in the circumstances.

Buy yourself time by creating the apparent need to refer back to someone else. Then when you go back you can review the situation to discover if the customer's thinking has changed. If not, you can now introduce some of the other variables, making sure that you get something extra in return.

For some years, I operated this principle with a friend of mine who runs a training business similar to my own. His areas of expertise are different, yet complementary, to mine so we frequently found ourselves working together with clients, covering different aspects of the business.

I know that when I needed some breathing space I would tell my client that I needed to refer back to my 'colleague'. Similarly I know that he occasionally said that he would need to refer back to me. Neither was the case because we ran our own completely independent companies, but by using this tactic we were able to manage the situation so that we could get the best out of our negotiations with customers.

In truth, this was more than a 'ploy' on both of our parts, because it did give us the opportunity to discuss situations with each other and seek advice on the best tactical approach to take.

SUMMARY

- When *negotiating* with customers – don't do it with one hand tied behind your back.

- *Agree the variables* with your boss and decide the ones you have authority to use.

- Follow the *guidelines for successful negotiating*.

- Try not to get backed into a corner, but if you get backed into a corner – *devise ways of getting back out.*

8

Consolidating your position and securing your future

Securing support from within your own organisation

If you reflect back to all of the good work that you have carried out in putting together your business MAP, you will realise that in the areas where you lose part of your existing customer base to your competition, the reasons will often have little to do with your own activities. There will be areas where it has been down to you, but I'm sure you're already working on these or you wouldn't have read this far.

What you need to do is identify the reasons why you are losing this business, perhaps it is:

- Poor service?
- Poor after sales customer care?
- Poor product quality?
- Poor response to customer complaints?
- Poor delivery?
- Unreasonable demands from some of your customer's people?

For these and any other reasons that you identify, you need to take the appropriate action, because, and I make no apology for repeating myself, it has to be easier to hold on to what you have than to constantly find new customers.

Consider where the problem lies and how to address it, but in so doing adopt the attitude that within your own organisation you are both a customer and a supplier. For those parts of your organisation which supply you with information and services to enable you to function at your best and bring in the results, you are the customer. Similarly you are the supplier to all of those people in your organisation who need accurate information from you to be able to perform their jobs satisfactorily.

170

You are the customer to the secretarial pool which produces your letters, proposals and other correspondence. You are also the supplier in that they can only do this if your requests are reasonable, understandable and made with sufficient notice being given.

You are the customer of the production department which makes the things that you sell – including samples. You are their supplier when they need accurate information to be able to make what you have sold. You are the customer of the distribution department which makes sure that the customers' goods are delivered in line with your promises. You are their supplier with the responsibility of ensuring that these delivery requests are reasonable and that the information you provide is clear and concise

You are the customer of the quality assurance and quality control departments which make sure that the goods which are delivered are in line with the specification you sold to the customer. You are their supplier and need to ensure that the specification you submit is within the scope of the company's abilities and that such specifications are clearly spelled out.

You are the customer of the service department which provides the back up so that your promises to the customer are kept. You are a good supplier when the promises you have made to your external customers are reasonable and in times of emergency, achievable.

You are also the supplier of information to your management team who need:

- Accurate forecasts on which to base their purchasing, manufacture or logistics scheduling.

- Goods and services sold in line with company policies and practices.

- Accurate paperwork to enable all of the departments to give of their best – and this includes the ability to submit invoices in line with your 'negotiated' contract. Don't blame the sales ledger department for getting it wrong if you didn't advise them of a change in price.

171

One of the secrets of success in all of these areas is good communication. Make sure that you give your colleagues all that they need in order to be able to give you all that you need.

But the real key to success here is an attitudinal one! Make sure that you:

- Don't make unreasonable demands.

- Don't order people about – even if you are the 'star' sales person or even the managing director.

- Don't leave every request to the last minute – give people time to prepare.

- Don't whinge. You don't like rude or constantly complaining customers – don't become the same for someone else.

- Don't allow your customers' people to take a bad attitude with your company's people. Become your own people's champion.

Every single thing that you do in your organisation should be done with a smile on your face, politeness in your manner and pleasantness in your tone. It will get you a lot further than any other type of attitude and working with you will become a pleasure. You will soon find that you can move mountains if your people enjoy working with you. My personal policy for moving mountains was always to make it appear that people were doing me favours and I found that they did.

172

In the course of my business I spend a great deal of my time living in hotels. In fact, in a busy year I will spend more time living in hotels than I will living in my own home. For that reason the quality of service which I get is extremely important to me and I know that I am a valuable hotels' customer. Not only because I live in hotels but also because my clients often accept my recommendations with regard to which hotels to use.

A few years ago, I was staying at the Coach House Hotel in Newport Pagnell in England which is one of the Lansbury Hotels, part of the Whitbread Group. During this stay, I was joined for a drink one evening by the managing director of Lansbury Hotels, Nigel Greenwood, who was on one of his regular visits to the various hotels under his control. I had met Nigel on a number of occasions when I was using Lansbury Hotels and his comments to me on that occasion took me somewhat by surprise.

He told me that in the course of his travels he had discovered that I was known on first-name terms in all of his hotels which I used. He also told me that in those hotels, I was by far and away their favourite customer and added, 'Do you know that the staff in these hotels will do anything for you!'

'I was so intrigued by this' he continued, 'that I tried to find out why. What I discovered was that the staff all regarded you as the *ultimate professional guest*. Any time you want something done you make them feel as if they are doing you a favour. You thank them when they do things for you, things that are yours as of right. When things go wrong you accept that they can go wrong and pleasantly and politely ask for them to be put right. Then you thank them when they are put right.

173

'You never raise your voice, you don't complain – you simply ask for improvement. You always smile, you always take some time out to chat about how things are going, you always appear to be interested in them as people and you're never unreasonable. In fact, I recently found out that on one occasion, when the trouser press in your room had broken down, one of the staff volunteered to press your clothes in time for your meeting the following day!'

I tell you this story, not to 'blow my own trumpet', but to try to get you to understand that if you adopt a similar attitude with the people with whom you work, they will do anything for you. At the end of the day you will need all the assistance you can get to bring in the results.

People hate bullies and complainers – don't become one.

Having given some thought to getting the best from your 'internal' customers and suppliers, let us now look at how you can consolidate your position with your 'external' customers.

LETTERS AND PROPOSALS – THE SILENT SALES PEOPLE

You will find that there are occasions when you are unable to get the decision without some kind of formal offer or proposal. You will also find that there are times when these will be read by your customer in your absence. I have always recommended that, where the business was significant to your company, these letters and proposals should be taken to the customer on a return appointment when you can go over the details of your offer with the customer.

The importance of letters is such that if I may I would like to start at the beginning of the sales cycle – your initial appointment. You should have a standard confirmation letter to remind your prospect or customer of the meeting and its purpose.

Something along the lines of the following:

Dear Mrs Jones

Further to our telephone conversation today I would like to confirm our arrangement to meet at your office on Thursday 2nd September at 10.00 a.m.

As the purpose of this meeting is to discuss our new range of contact lenses, I would welcome the attendance of any of your colleagues for whom you believe our meeting may hold some interest.

Yours sincerely

Simple and straightforward, it confirms the date, time and location. It also reminds the prospect or customer of the purpose of the meeting and invites the participation of other parts of the decision-making process (DMP).

The letter which submits your offer on the basis of your previous meeting, whether taken or sent should be the real 'silent sales person', i.e. it should be good enough to do the selling for you if you aren't present at the time it's being read.

The key points of the letter should be:

1 To summarise the agreement regarding the identified needs and desires of the customer, while reminding the customer, if appropriate, that he or she agreed with that summary.

2 To link your offer or recommendations to the summary, while introducing, or hopefully restating, the benefits to the customer of accepting your recommendations.

3 To conclude with an assumptive request for the order.

Other points which are important are:

■ The language should be in the third person and should not be egocentric – use we instead of I.

■ The language should be passive, it's less confrontational. So, use expressions like 'the understanding taken from our meeting is . . .' instead of 'you told us that . . .'.

■ Write as you would speak – don't use the word 'ascertain' if you would normally say 'find out'. Conversely if you would say 'ascertain', don't write 'find out'.

■ Include in the letter the type of expressions that the customer used. It helps your customer to recognise that you understand his or her business.

It may be that in your business the practice is to submit a standardised quotation. If that is the case, send a covering letter to make sure that you remind the customer about the meeting and the agreed information which came from it.

I recall an occasion when I had a meeting to discuss sales training with a large firm of Commercial Property managers and estate agents. During the course of this meeting, my contact said, 'You have to understand that our people are professionals in the truest sense of the word, in that they are surveyors, valuers etc., so the American hard sell approach would be inappropriate'.

To be honest, his statement annoyed me, although I didn't let it show, because I firmly believe that there are few occupations as professional as good selling. When I took my proposal along to our return meeting, part of it read, 'Bearing in mind that your people are professionals in the truest sense of the word, we believe that an American style hard sell approach would be singularly inappropriate. With this in mind we would recommend . . .'

As my contact was reading this through, he stopped and remarked, 'You know, Mr Cowden, you obviously understand our business. I could have said that myself'.

Only if he reads this book will he learn that he did!

There will be occasions when you will need to submit a more detailed and possibly more lengthy proposal than a one- or two-page letter. What I would like to give you here is a tried and tested format for such proposals which I use almost as standard in my own business, even if the proposal only contains three or four pages:

1 Produce a front cover and give the proposal a professional appearance and an identity.

176

2 Begin with a section which outlines the background surrounding the proposal.

3 The second section should outline the key points from the discussion, including a summary of the agreed needs in the meeting.

4 The third section should contain your recommendations, based on and linked to the summary. Within this section there should also be the statement, or restatement, of the benefits for the customer of accepting your recommendations.

Note: It is also within this section that, if it is appropriate to your business, you will include the price. There are two reasons why it should be here:

177

(i) You will be able to link the price to the benefits, creating a value for money link between the benefits and your price.

(ii) The customer will need to read the whole proposal to discover the price. You might think this is quite sneaky, but it's not any more doubtful than the customer who receives your proposal and immediately turns to the back page to find out the price, without giving any regard to the rest of the proposal which you so carefully prepared.

5 The final section should be the conclusion, within which you will ask for the order.

6 If it is necessary, you could include a section on your company, together with the enclosure of your company's standard terms of business.

When all of this has been done, have it bound. There are a number of alternative methods of doing this, all of which are fairly inexpensive. The resulting professional effect is worth the time and money.

Let us now turn our attention to the 'after sales' letter. There are a number of standard approaches to this type of letter, basically all suggesting that about a month after the sale, you write thanking the customer for the purchase, enquiring as to how satisfactory it has been, introducing other similar products and inviting the customer to contact you personally if he or she thinks that you can be of further service.

All of these letters have a degree of success, but many will end up in the waste basket. I would like you to think about being a little more original in your approach. Try to think of some inexpensive way of getting some real impact from your 'after sales' letter. After all the real purpose of the letter is to maintain contact and hopefully get the customer to buy more.

Some years ago I bought a Volvo car from the local dealer in my area. A month after I had bought the car, I received the almost standard 'after sales letter' – except this one contained a small tin of touch up paint to match the car. Later, the same Volvo dealer sent **the car** a birthday card! I never forgot who had sold me that car.

For the majority of you who are in field sales, the likelihood is that you won't need to send these types of correspondence because you will be in regular contact with your customers. If it is a feature of your business, be a little more creative than your competition. Similarly, don't write to a customer that hasn't ordered for a while, call them up and arrange an appointment.

BUILDING CUSTOMER LOYALTY

The real secret of building customer loyalty is to recognise that it isn't only down to the sales people, it's a total company issue. So you may have to enlist the help of the other members of your organisation who could or perhaps should have contact with your customers.

The first step in ensuring that your customers remain loyal to you, even when the competition is knocking on their door is to build up the personal relationship which exists between you and the customer. Then, of course, you need to make sure that the goods and services you supply are in line with the customer's expectations.

Within your core business, try to become involved in **multi-level contact**. The principle of multi-level contact is to establish a series of relationships at various levels in the organisational pyramid, whereby members of your organisation are involved directly with members of your customer's organisation.

Get your manager to meet your contact and your contact's boss. If you have a secretary, establish contact between your secretary and your contact's secretary or assistant. Get your engineers to talk to their engineers, your designers to talk to their production people, your quality control to talk to their quality assurance etc.

This will ensure that if ever there is a problem, there will be more points of reference between your two companies to take the heat out of any potentially threatening situation. It will also mean that the competition will find it more difficult to replace you, because there will be a number of people in your customer's company who have established a 'comfort

179

zone' of working with your company and will not want to change that.

I worked with a large refrigeration company some years ago who had established just such a situation with their major customer; one of the largest food retailers in the UK. Such was the success of the relationship, that not only were the competition unable to put them out of the stores where they were established, they couldn't prevent them from securing the work which came about from the building of new stores.

In addition to multi-level contact, there is another way to build customer loyalty – get them to help you expand your business!

REFERRALS AND PREFERRALS

A **referral** is where you get your customer to recommend that you get in touch with another company with a view to getting their business too. These could be among friends, suppliers, perhaps even competitors where there would be no conflicting interests. What would then happen is that you would make contact with the new company, using your customer's name, and set up a meeting to discuss doing business. This has a very high success rate.

There is a better way – I call it a preferral.

A **preferral** is where the customer calls the other company to suggest that they meet with you. These situations aren't too common, yet more common than you would believe, and when they happen, the success rate is phenomenal!

I have literally built my own business on the basis of both

referrals and preferrals. In chapter 2, I mentioned how this system had been put in place with one of my clients, a large insurance company. I recall doing some field accompaniment with one of their sales people, who specifically asked me to show him how to get these referrals and, if possible, preferrals.

We arrived at one of his appointments, which was some further business he had arranged with one of his existing customers. During the course of the conversation, I listened as the customer was explaining the need for the new insurance cover. It turned out that he was a joiner who had been employed by a company supplying fitted kitchens. His job along with some of his colleagues was the actual installation. The reason for the change in his insurance circumstances came about because he and four other workers had secured the installation contract for another kitchen company and they had set up their own business to carry out this work.

181

When the original business had been completed and we were enjoying a cup of coffee, I quietly asked him about the other people with whom he had set up business; what they did, where they lived, how similar their circumstances were etc. When I was given this information, I asked if he thought that it would be a good idea for these people to be contacted, which he did.

As the sales person was eagerly writing down the names and telephone numbers of the other four people, I quietly said to the customer, 'I'm sure you appreciate that it can be difficult to get to see people in this business and I'm sure that you wouldn't want your friends to be disturbed if they genuinely weren't interested.' He agreed, so I continued, 'Well, I wonder if it would be possible for you to give them a quick call to make sure that we wouldn't be unwelcome?'

'That's a good idea', he said, and proceeded to call each of them on the telephone. He set up meetings there and then with three of them but one of them wasn't interested.

What happened next surprised me. He sat with his wife trying to think of other people whom they knew whose situation may have been right for the insurance sales person to call, and he didn't give up until about half an hour later he had succeeded in setting up a fourth appointment. It was almost as if having originally given us four names, he was determined to set up four appointments. Due to the way that these had been set up, the success rate on the appointments was 100 per cent.

The important thing to remember is that, if you have managed to get one of your customers to help you build your business, their perception of the goods or services you supply must be such that they are happy for other people to associate their name with them. In addition, you must have established a good relationship with the customer for you to get the referral or preferral in the first place. Often, getting these from customers can be quite straightforward, it's just that it never occurs to most of us to try.

In some of your businesses it will also be possible for you to get these from prospects to whom you have failed to sell – particularly if the reason was that, at that time, they really didn't have a need to buy what you were offering. If you had good rapport with the prospect and they liked what you had to offer, but they just didn't need it, they will often give you advice regarding who could use your products or services. All you have to do is ask, people are naturally helpful.

Another crucial way of securing your future is to be alert to what your competition is doing. So let us look at gathering *competitor intelligence*.

Back in chapter 1, I suggested that the field sales force should not be used to gather any in depth market research or information. This does not however apply to competitor intelligence.

Here are a few questions for you:

- Who are the companies competing with you on your territory?
- What is their sales turnover compared to your company's?
- What size are they in relation to your company?
- What are the sizes of their field sales forces?
- Do you know any of the competitor sales people's names?
- What are their pricing and discounting policies?
- What type of marketing promotions do they employ?
- What are the major differences between their products and yours?
- Do you know the salary levels of their sales people?
- What kind of cars do they drive?
- What are their general reputations with customers and prospects?
- What new products have they recently launched?
- Do you know if their sales people are regularly trained?

This is the type of information that you need to feed back to your management team in order that you can keep one step ahead of your competition.

The final area I would like to address with regard to securing your future is your own **Personal** and **Career Development**.

If you refer back to the diagram in chapter 1, securing the sales results, we are about to complete **Steps 7** and **8**. The first thing you have to do is analyse your own qualifications, i.e. the areas of knowledge and skill that are needed to successfully do the job. I have provided a list of some of the subjects that ought to be included, based on my work with some of my own clients, but this is not exhaustive. You will need to develop your own list relating to your business and perhaps you may elicit the help of a manager or colleague in putting this list together.

Let's begin with the *knowledge areas* listed in Table 8.1.

If you look at the area that refers to the range of products/services, you may have to break these further down into specific groups. Similarly in the area that refers to knowledge of your competitors, you may want to add some items in addition to the questions I asked of you in the section on competitor intelligence.

Now we'll look at the predominantly *skill areas* listed in Table 8.2.

If you are a sales manager reading this section, there is a supplement that has been designed especially for you – see Table 8.3.

When you have finalised your list of knowledge and skill areas, rate yourself on a scale of 1 to 20, 20 being excellence bordering on perfection. The next thing you may have to do is try to be objective and rate each of the items on the basis of the levels demanded by the job. It could well be that you're new in selling and your levels are still being developed.

There is one thing I would like you to make special note of, that where your qualifications are already in excess of that demanded by the job. This is usually an area where you are particularly comfortable. Beware that in these situations you may indulge yourself in too much of that type of activity at the expense of something more important.

One of the classics which springs to mind is report writing. I mentioned in my introduction that sales people hate paperwork. Whenever I have come across a sales person who enjoys, and is therefore good at, paperwork, I have found that at times when they are under pressure, they have a tendency to hide themselves in paperwork. It doesn't mean that if you do enjoy paperwork that this will happen, but it is worth watching for.

185

Select the three or four areas where the difference between what is *needed* and what *exists* is greatest and create a **personal development plan**, similar to Table 8.4.

The time scale for the 'from' and 'to' should be six months. Thereafter you will be able to create a rolling six-month development plan. Limit the number of areas to three or four, otherwise you won't be able to complete the plan and continue bringing in the results.

When you have filled in the areas for development on the plan, consider what you may have to do to bring about the achievement:

- Study some books?
- Attend a training course?
- Work with a colleague, etc?

Table 8.1 Personal development profile: areas of knowledge

Knowledge of your Own Company:	1	2	3	4	5	6	7	8	9	10	11	12	13	14	15	16	17	18	19	20
The Structure of the Company	1	2	3	4	5	6	7	8	9	10	11	12	13	14	15	16	17	18	19	20
The History of the Company	1	2	3	4	5	6	7	8	9	10	11	12	13	14	15	16	17	18	19	20
The Corporate Objectives	1	2	3	4	5	6	7	8	9	10	11	12	13	14	15	16	17	18	19	20
The Product Strategies	1	2	3	4	5	6	7	8	9	10	11	12	13	14	15	16	17	18	19	20
New Product Development	1	2	3	4	5	6	7	8	9	10	11	12	13	14	15	16	17	18	19	20
The Company's Share of the Market	1	2	3	4	5	6	7	8	9	10	11	12	13	14	15	16	17	18	19	20
Knowledge of the Product/Services:																				
The Range of Products/Services	1	2	3	4	5	6	7	8	9	10	11	12	13	14	15	16	17	18	19	20
How the products work	1	2	3	4	5	6	7	8	9	10	11	12	13	14	15	16	17	18	19	20
How they are made	1	2	3	4	5	6	7	8	9	10	11	12	13	14	15	16	17	18	19	20
The Materials and Design	1	2	3	4	5	6	7	8	9	10	11	12	13	14	15	16	17	18	19	20
Their position against the competition	1	2	3	4	5	6	7	8	9	10	11	12	13	14	15	16	17	18	19	20
The Pricing Structure	1	2	3	4	5	6	7	8	9	10	11	12	13	14	15	16	17	18	19	20
The Sales Terms	1	2	3	4	5	6	7	8	9	10	11	12	13	14	15	16	17	18	19	20
The Warranty Conditions	1	2	3	4	5	6	7	8	9	10	11	12	13	14	15	16	17	18	19	20
The Service Terms	1	2	3	4	5	6	7	8	9	10	11	12	13	14	15	16	17	18	19	20
Knowledge of the Market																				
The Size of the Market	1	2	3	4	5	6	7	8	9	10	11	12	13	14	15	16	17	18	19	20
The Trends in the Market	1	2	3	4	5	6	7	8	9	10	11	12	13	14	15	16	17	18	19	20

The Customer Profile	1	2	3	4	5	6	7	8	9	10	11	12	13	14	15	16	17	18	19	20
Environmental Forces	1	2	3	4	5	6	7	8	9	10	11	12	13	14	15	16	17	18	19	20
Government Regulations	1	2	3	4	5	6	7	8	9	10	11	12	13	14	15	16	17	18	19	20

Knowledge of your own Customers:

The Buying Policy	1	2	3	4	5	6	7	8	9	10	11	12	13	14	15	16	17	18	19	20
The Decision Making Process	1	2	3	4	5	6	7	8	9	10	11	12	13	14	15	16	17	18	19	20
Buying Patterns	1	2	3	4	5	6	7	8	9	10	11	12	13	14	15	16	17	18	19	20
Affiliations to other Companies or Buying Groups	1	2	3	4	5	6	7	8	9	10	11	12	13	14	15	16	17	18	19	20
Terms and Conditions of Contract	1	2	3	4	5	6	7	8	9	10	11	12	13	14	15	16	17	18	19	20

Knowledge of your Competitors:

The Ownership (part of a group)	1	2	3	4	5	6	7	8	9	10	11	12	13	14	15	16	17	18	19	20
The Product Range	1	2	3	4	5	6	7	8	9	10	11	12	13	14	15	16	17	18	19	20
Strengths or Weaknesses of the Products	1	2	3	4	5	6	7	8	9	10	11	12	13	14	15	16	17	18	19	20
Strengths or Weaknesses of the Pricing Policies	1	2	3	4	5	6	7	8	9	10	11	12	13	14	15	16	17	18	19	20
Their Penetration with your Customers	1	2	3	4	5	6	7	8	9	10	11	12	13	14	15	16	17	18	19	20
Their Core Business	1	2	3	4	5	6	7	8	9	10	11	12	13	14	15	16	17	18	19	20

Table 8.2 Personal development profile: areas of skill

Telephone Appointment Making:

	1	2	3	4	5	6	7	8	9	10	11	12	13	14	15	16	17	18	19	20
Overcoming Objections	1	2	3	4	5	6	7	8	9	10	11	12	13	14	15	16	17	18	19	20
Closing Techniques	1	2	3	4	5	6	7	8	9	10	11	12	13	14	15	16	17	18	19	20

Selling Skills when 'Face to Face':

	1	2	3	4	5	6	7	8	9	10	11	12	13	14	15	16	17	18	19	20
Your Own and Company Introduction	1	2	3	4	5	6	7	8	9	10	11	12	13	14	15	16	17	18	19	20
Establishing the DMP	1	2	3	4	5	6	7	8	9	10	11	12	13	14	15	16	17	18	19	20
Questioning Skills	1	2	3	4	5	6	7	8	9	10	11	12	13	14	15	16	17	18	19	20
Note Taking	1	2	3	4	5	6	7	8	9	10	11	12	13	14	15	16	17	18	19	20
Other Information Gathering Skills	1	2	3	4	5	6	7	8	9	10	11	12	13	14	15	16	17	18	19	20
Identifying Needs and Desires	1	2	3	4	5	6	7	8	9	10	11	12	13	14	15	16	17	18	19	20
Summarising	1	2	3	4	5	6	7	8	9	10	11	12	13	14	15	16	17	18	19	20
Presenting your Recommendations	1	2	3	4	5	6	7	8	9	10	11	12	13	14	15	16	17	18	19	20
Presenting Price	1	2	3	4	5	6	7	8	9	10	11	12	13	14	15	16	17	18	19	20
Handling Objections	1	2	3	4	5	6	7	8	9	10	11	12	13	14	15	16	17	18	19	20
Closing the Sale	1	2	3	4	5	6	7	8	9	10	11	12	13	14	15	16	17	18	19	20
Winning Commitment to the Next Stage	1	2	3	4	5	6	7	8	9	10	11	12	13	14	15	16	17	18	19	20

	1	2	3	4	5	6	7	8	9	10	11	12	13	14	15	16	17	18	19	20
Keeping Control	1	2	3	4	5	6	7	8	9	10	11	12	13	14	15	16	17	18	19	20
Body Language	1	2	3	4	5	6	7	8	9	10	11	12	13	14	15	16	17	18	19	20
Presenting to Groups	1	2	3	4	5	6	7	8	9	10	11	12	13	14	15	16	17	18	19	20
Establishing Rapport	1	2	3	4	5	6	7	8	9	10	11	12	13	14	15	16	17	18	19	20

Other Areas of Knowledge and Skill:

	1	2	3	4	5	6	7	8	9	10	11	12	13	14	15	16	17	18	19	20
Knowlege of your own Area	1	2	3	4	5	6	7	8	9	10	11	12	13	14	15	16	17	18	19	20
Territory Management	1	2	3	4	5	6	7	8	9	10	11	12	13	14	15	16	17	18	19	20
Letter and Proposal Writing	1	2	3	4	5	6	7	8	9	10	11	12	13	14	15	16	17	18	19	20
Report Writing	1	2	3	4	5	6	7	8	9	10	11	12	13	14	15	16	17	18	19	20
Personal Administration	1	2	3	4	5	6	7	8	9	10	11	12	13	14	15	16	17	18	19	20
Pre-call Planning	1	2	3	4	5	6	7	8	9	10	11	12	13	14	15	16	17	18	19	20
Cyclical Call Planning	1	2	3	4	5	6	7	8	9	10	11	12	13	14	15	16	17	18	19	20

189

Table 8.3 Supplement for managers

Management Areas of Knowledge and Skill:

	1	2	3	4	5	6	7	8	9	10	11	12	13	14	15	16	17	18	19	20
Team Leadership	1	2	3	4	5	6	7	8	9	10	11	12	13	14	15	16	17	18	19	20
Decision Making	1	2	3	4	5	6	7	8	9	10	11	12	13	14	15	16	17	18	19	20
Problem Solving	1	2	3	4	5	6	7	8	9	10	11	12	13	14	15	16	17	18	19	20
Coaching	1	2	3	4	5	6	7	8	9	10	11	12	13	14	15	16	17	18	19	20
Counselling	1	2	3	4	5	6	7	8	9	10	11	12	13	14	15	16	17	18	19	20
Performance Appraisal	1	2	3	4	5	6	7	8	9	10	11	12	13	14	15	16	17	18	19	20
Conducting Field Accompaniment	1	2	3	4	5	6	7	8	9	10	11	12	13	14	15	16	17	18	19	20
Training in the Field	1	2	3	4	5	6	7	8	9	10	11	12	13	14	15	16	17	18	19	20
Training in the Classroom	1	2	3	4	5	6	7	8	9	10	11	12	13	14	15	16	17	18	19	20
Running Effective Sales Meetings	1	2	3	4	5	6	7	8	9	10	11	12	13	14	15	16	17	18	19	20
Objective Setting	1	2	3	4	5	6	7	8	9	10	11	12	13	14	15	16	17	18	19	20
Exhibition Management	1	2	3	4	5	6	7	8	9	10	11	12	13	14	15	16	17	18	19	20
Financial Awareness	1	2	3	4	5	6	7	8	9	10	11	12	13	14	15	16	17	18	19	20
Budgeting, Targeting and Forecasting	1	2	3	4	5	6	7	8	9	10	11	12	13	14	15	16	17	18	19	20
Recruitment and Induction of Sales People	1	2	3	4	5	6	7	8	9	10	11	12	13	14	15	16	17	18	19	20
Inter-departmental Communication	1	2	3	4	5	6	7	8	9	10	11	12	13	14	15	16	17	18	19	20
Account Management	1	2	3	4	5	6	7	8	9	10	11	12	13	14	15	16	17	18	19	20
Stress Management – in your Team*	1	2	3	4	5	6	7	8	9	10	11	12	13	14	15	16	17	18	19	20

Table 8.4 Personal Development Plan (PDP)

PERSONAL DEVELOPMENT PLAN			From		To	
Area for Development	Action for Achievement	Resource	Start Date	Review Date	Standard Desired	

Now consider the resources that you may have to call on:

- Will your company send you on a course?
- Do they have a distance learning library?
- Can you find what you're looking for in a public library?

Note: I think that it's important to recognise here that the examples which I have given as options, in reality, aren't alternatives.

Reading books is great, but it's only part of the solution. There is no substitute for training being carried out in an environment where ideas can be shared or even challenged. Where someone can demonstrate the skills and explain the finer points of ideas. Similarly, on the job, training is vital, where a colleague or manager can show by example or can observe you in action to be able to give you feed back on how well you are developing.

Now set a start date for each activity, making them different start dates within the period. Also, set a review date when you will check your progress, and make a note of the current standard and the one you wish to achieve during the time allowed. Remember not to expect too much. If you chose an area where your level was 11, don't expect to move from 11 to 18 in one step. Create stages, and aim for 14 as a first step. On your second six-month plan you will be able to aim for the next improvement.

When all of this has been done, make a copy of your Personal Development Plan and give that copy to someone very close to you. The reason is simple; you need to know that someone else will recognise if you have broken a promise you made to yourself!

In my supplement for managers, you may have noticed that I put an asterisk beside the item 'Stress Management – in your Team'. The reason for this is that recent research suggests that there are a number of people who actually thrive on stress and that these can usually be found at the top in their chosen profession.

If that is the case, perhaps it is more important for a manager to consider the various things which cause stress in her or his people. Good management practice can reduce the incidence of stress in people, so I have concentrated here on that aspect of stress management rather than on addressing it in the manager.

193

Whenever I have conducted graduate training courses with companies such as SmithKline Beecham or The Ciba Group, I include a session which I entitle 'The Psychology of Success' and this personal development plan is a part of that session.

I work with groups of around 21 to 25 people in these sessions and I usually tell them that in a group of that size there will only be two or three people who will do something about carrying out their personal development plan. Whenever I have occasion to meet them after the programme, perhaps when I am visiting the facility where they work, I always ask them what they did about their plan. Unfortunately, whenever this occurs, my original thinking is borne out.

Thankfully, however, there have been a few real successes which encourage me to keep up the good work.

Like David, who already had a First Class Honours Degree but felt that it would be worthwhile studying for an MBA.

The problem was that while he was prepared to pay the physical and psychological price of studying, he couldn't afford the financial cost of the exercise. When he spoke to me about this, I suggested that he contact his personnel manager to seek the company's help with the course fees. He told me that it was a general policy that his company didn't do that sort of thing. I suggested that he put the idea forward anyway.

He took my advice, agreed to make the commitment of time and effort, and his company agreed to make the financial commitment!

Like Lorraine, who during one of these sessions took me aside and said that regarding my question about enjoying what you do and what you would rather be doing, she had a problem. It transpired that she had left another company to work with her current one and recognised that for her it was a bad decision and that she would rather be back at the old company. I suggested that she call the old company and ask to speak to the personnel manager. Her reply was that it was a company policy not to rehire people who had left the company for other employment.

I suggested again that she make the call and told her that if she was really good enough, yet they wouldn't take her back, then *the tail had started to wag the dog* and her old company weren't really the type of people that she thought they were and she should look elsewhere. I didn't find out what had happened until about a year later when I was visiting the facility of her old company and met her in the staff restaurant.

Now, I meet a few hundred new people each year and while I am very good with faces, the names tend to escape me – confounded by the fact that most people tend to wear their identity badges hooked to the belt of their trousers or skirts. Let me tell you that it can do tremendous harm to your reputation to be seen constantly wandering around a facility staring at people's thighs and hips!

Anyway, when I met Lorraine she said to me, 'You don't remember me, do you?' 'Yes', I replied. 'You were on one of the graduate programmes last year'. 'That's right', she said. 'But not with this company.' She then reminded me about the situation I have just described, and it came about that she did make the phone call and they did take her back, so she was happy and obviously so were her employers, or they wouldn't have taken her back in the first place.

Or, in a similar vein, Sharon, who recognised that what she was doing for a living was not what she would really prefer to be doing, so made a career shift, sacrificing a considerable amount by way of salary, to move into a different area of business entirely. She studied for new qualifications and actively sought out employment in the new business area and things appear to be progressing satisfactorily.

195

Not all of the people mentioned have totally made it yet, but I firmly believe that having made the commitment in the first place they will ALL come out well in the end! I hope, too, that the fact that you have actively chosen to read and work your way through this book will mean that your chances of doing something really concrete with your own plan will be considerably higher than the average and that you may emulate the stories which I have just related.

If you do make a real success of it, write and let me know.

Finally, let me spend a little more time talking about *career development* by introducing you to the **Psychology of Success**.

To make this work to maximum effect, you will need to begin by taking some notepaper and carrying out some self-analysis.

Here is a short exercise for you:

1 List three goals you have set and achieved in the past.

Anyone who has a professional qualification or a university degree etc., will be immediately able to identify at least one. Don't give up at *one*, if you're old enough to be in selling, you will have achieved at least three, perhaps including getting your current job.

2 List your three most important career goals – at this moment.

It could be promotion, or a change of job or being Top Sales Person. If you want to be successful, you will have them!

3 List your three most important personal or family goals – at this moment.

Remember that it's very easy when you're concentrating on business to forget that you have a family – DON'T.

4 List your three most important financial goals – at this moment.

Perhaps you want to buy a new car, have a special holiday or buy a new house.

5 If it was possible to guarantee success in any one endeavour – what would it be?

Remember that goals or objectives are measurable, achievable and time-oriented.

6 Name three people at the top of your field right now –
then list what you think you could learn from them.

There are people at the top of every profession – to be
successful you should know who they are.

7 Make a note of what you are currently doing about exercise 6, above.

8 Make a list of the business, management or technical
magazines or books which you actively seek out and study
– even if you only study parts of them.

9 How many books do you read – on average?

Per Year? Per Month? Per Week?

10 Of these, how many are fiction and how many non-fiction?

11 What made you decide to get into the selling business?

12 Is what you do for a living the most fun you can have with
your clothes on?

13 If not, what would you rather be doing for a living?

14 If you have answered NO to 12 above, and have been able
to give an answer to 13, what positive steps can you take
to bring this about?

I said at the beginning of the exercise that it was a short
one. However, if you spent any less than half an hour on it,
you didn't think deeply enough – or maybe your desire to be
successful isn't as great as you think it is? Remember, however, irrespective of your personal definition of success, **your
ultimate aim is to be happy and fulfilled!**

If the point of some of my questions in that exercise wasn't
clear, it soon should be.

I would now like to give you my Ten-Point Plan for success!

1 You will need to **develop self discipline** to achieve everything you want in your career. Don't follow the 'line of least resistance' – discipline is the cornerstone of success.

2 Make sure that you have **purpose** in your life – set yourself *meaningful, stretching goals.*

First, **decide what you want** from your career. Then *determine the price* that you will have to pay. This price isn't necessarily in monetary terms, it is more likely to be the time and effort you will need to devote to achieving what you want. It will also include sacrificing some of the things that you enjoy – albeit short term. Finally, you then have to *commit to paying the price* – otherwise it won't work.

I always found that a bit of 'backward planning' helped me. If you can determine what it is you want, you can usually work backwards to identify what it is that you have to do to get it.

3 **Strive for excellence.** Try to be the *best* at what you do. Use successful people you know as role models – or at worst try to learn from the mistakes of others. Surround yourself with successful people and, if published, read their books.

There's a wonderful, appropriate American expression which says, *'Don't mix with the turkeys – fly with the eagles!'*

In *'Up the Organisation'*, Robert Townsend says, 'If you can't do it excellently, don't do it at all. Because if it's not excellent it won't be profitable or fun, and if you're not in business for fun or profit, what the hell are you doing here?'

The real secret of success is to **find what you like doing best – then find someone who'll pay you for doing it!**

4 Hold yourself **responsible for your own success**. Don't blame other people if things don't go right. Stop making excuses to yourself and get rid of this notion of *Luck*! Believe me, the harder and smarter you work the luckier you will become.

5 **Concentrate on your self development** – the responsibility is yours. On a daily basis I come across people who think that because their formal education is complete they have learned all that they need to. I have a simple test for anyone who wants to know if their learning is complete. Hold a mirror in front of your mouth and if the mirror mists up because you're breathing – your learning hasn't yet finished!

In all the years of my career, among the top people in industry and commerce that I have met, I have discovered that there is one thing they all have in common; quite simply – *they know more than the rest of us*!

6 **Practice creativity.** Earlier in this book I referred to the creativity of sales peoples' call reports and expense claims; this isn't what I mean here. Work on the principle that there is a better way of doing things than at present and constantly be looking for that better way. You only need to be a little better than your competition to be considerably more successful.

Don't subscribe to the school of mediocrity that believes; 'If it isn't broken – don't fix it!'

7 **Don't give up** – there will be setbacks. If it was easy everyone would be doing it – which would probably

cause you to redefine the criteria for success. So have courage and be persistent.

8 **Work and co-operate with others.** You won't be able to do it entirely alone. You will need help and co-operation from your loved ones and your colleagues.

9 **Have integrity and be honest.** Lord Forté, who founded the Trust House Forté Hotel and Catering Chain (THF), is quoted in Edward de Bono's book, *'Tactics: the Art and Science of Success'* as saying, 'You must be able to go anywhere in the world and know there'll be no one there who can point a finger and say – that man did me down!'

I'm sure that all of you reading this book can identify successful people you know, whose success is not begrudged by others while at the same time you will know successful people whose demise is anticipated with glee. If you don't practise honesty and integrity in your dealings with people, it won't be a question of them awaiting your downfall, they will be trying to help you fall all the way – and you'll deserve it! Business history, much of it recent, is littered with many deserving cases of 'come-uppance'.

10 **Be single minded.** You have to concentrate on the achievement of your own success. However, don't confuse *single-mindedness* with *selfishness*. That is as valid as confusing assertiveness with aggression.

Let me leave you with a couple of additional thoughts:

My good friend Derek Stables who retired recently as Director of Management Education and Training for Ciba-Geigy PLC used to say,

> 'The *only* place where **success** comes before **work**
> – is in a *dictionary*!'

From my own observations let me tell you that there are only four types of people:

- Those who *make things happen,*

- Those who *watch things happen,*

- Those who *wonder what happened,* and

- Those who are blissfully *unaware that anything ever did happen.*

In view of the fact that in reading this book you have involved yourself in a considerable amount of self-development, I would like to add the following:

201

Although ultimately the responsibility for developing yourself rests with you, you need to work for the kind of company that is prepared to help you. Think about the company you are with. Do they conduct regular training and development programmes for you? If not, go somewhere where you will get some real help in your desire to further your career.

I wrote earlier in this book about Tom Peters' attitude to training. Well I'm glad to say that he is not alone, albeit he may be, like me, in the minority. I had occasion about a year ago to meet with Gerard Eadie, the self-made businessman, who founded and built up C.R. Smith, the hugely successful double-glazing company. During our conversation he told me that his opinion was that his sales people should be retrained approximately every six months. I have to agree, not because that is my business, but because I know from bitter experience how easy it is to lose the 'golden touch'.

Absolutely finally.

The reason I asked you if you found selling the most fun you could have with your clothes on is quite simple. If you didn't answer positively, maybe you should think again.

> **This is a really tough business when you enjoy it: it will be sheer hell if you don't!**

SUMMARY

- Learn to secure the support of your own organisation; remember that you have 'internal' customers too.

- Identify why you lose customers and do something about it.

- Create letters and proposals that have the ability to sell in your absence.

- Build your customers' loyalty by every means at your disposal.

- Get your customers to help you build your business.

- Know who your competitors are, how they operate and their strengths and weaknesses – so that you can win over them.

- Analyse, honestly, your qualifications and create a personal development plan.

- Concentrate on your own career development.

- Develop The Psychology of Success!

In Conclusion

■

If you followed my advice in the introduction to this book you will probably have spent as much time working through it as I have writing it. If you have worked through the book I congratulate you because I know that it can't have been easy. If you flagged in the middle and began to skip through the various chapters picking out things that appeared more important to you in your own situation – that's all right too. However, if you do nothing else, make sure that you complete all of the work on Mapping the Business.

A number of my clients have commented on the fact that after working with my company, they seem to become a lot luckier. This has absolutely nothing to do with divine intervention, but a great deal to do with my firmly held belief that; **The Harder and Smarter you work – the Luckier you get!** Working smarter is all about being effective.

If you began to work your way through the book and your resolve failed you, give the book to someone else who may have more success with it – it will be a gift worth a fortune to the person who uses it. If you have any success stories, write to me and tell me about them. If something didn't work for you, write to me about these situations too – I may be able to offer some advice. Whatever you do, I hope you have enjoyed the experience even if it was hard work.

I began the book by being provocative because I knew that the nature of Sales People is such that you would be able to handle the provocation and perhaps even relate to some of my 'off the cuff' remarks. Those of us who are in Professional Selling are, in my opinion, truly the *crème de la crème*. Without us the economy of our companies and our countries would simply disintigrate.

There are times, however, when we are our own worst enemies; The popular perception of us is that we are overpaid and underworked. We drive around all day in our expensive company cars, wining and dining, wearing our Sunday best clothes and generally making people feel envious of us. We are smooth talkers who could charm the birds out of the trees. It's absolute rubbish, but it is what a lot of people believe. I often get the feeling when I'm talking to people in non sales departments of companies that this is exactly what they think. To be fair, in my case some of this is self-inflicted because I have never been a member of the 'shrinking violet' fraternity. The result is that when I am met with that reaction I usually make matters worse by reminding the people concerned that if people like me weren't selling the goods there would be no point in anyone else making them.

Be proud of your Profession; Nothing Happens Till Somebody Sells Something!

204

Bibliography

■

Up The Organisation by Robert Townsend (Hodder Fawcett, 1971)

Thriving on Chaos by Tom Peters (Macmillan Publishing, 1988)

Tactics: The Art & Science of Success by Edward De Bono (Harper Collins, 1986)

The Tom Peters Experience, The Customer Revolution by Tom Peters (Video Film, BBC Training Videos, 1989)

Pricing for Results by John Winkler (Heinemann Professional Publishing, 1991)

Marketing Management by Philip Kotler (Simon & Schuster, 8th Edition, 1994)

Competitive Strategy by Michael E Porter (Macmillan Publishing, 1980)

Stress Management Techniques by Dr. Vernon Coleman (W. H. Allen & Co, 1988)

The Ultimate USP is You by Jim Cowden (Pitman Publishing, 1994)

Index

■

ability to influence *see* AID
action plan 5, 6, 48, 75; *see also* direction of activity
activity plans 44, 51, 56, 58
'added value' 23
after-sales letter 178
aggressive questions 165
AID (Ability to Influence the Decision) 139–40
aims *see* targets
alertness on telephone 90
appointments: calling for *see* telephone calls; making skills 24–5, 31; to telephone ratio 57, 58–9; *see also* calls assumptive telephoning 93, 94
authority: negotiation with 158–66; responsibility without 153–4

backing out of corner 166, 167–8
backward planning to ensure future results 28–35
bargaining *see* negotiation
batteries 73
benefits of mapping the business 44–6
best call analysis 132
Bono, Edward de: *Tactics: the Art and Science of Success* 200
budgets 1–2
business MAP 7–11, 169; *see*

also quality of activity; quantity of activity

calculators 73
'call off' orders 156–7
calls: meaningful selling 39–41; post-call analysis 131–2, 150–51; pre-call planning 127–31, 134–7, 147–8; reporting system 78–81; *see also* cold calls; direction of activity; telephone calls car as mobile office 109–11
career development *see* personal and career development
Chamberlain, Peter 88
checking questions 161–2
Ciba Group 68, 98, 193, 200
classifying customers 67–9
'clover leaf' principle of territory management 57–63
Coats Patons 49
cold calls 51, 58, 83–7
Coleman, Vernon: *Stress Management techniques* 153
collection instead of delivery 157
competition, customers lost to 21–3
computers 115–17, 120–22
consolidating position and securing future ix, 169–203;

building customer loyalty 179–80; letters and proposals 174–8; personal and career development ix, 184–202; referrals and preferrals 180–83; support from within own organisation 169–74

conversion ratios: and direction of activity 52, 58; and quality of activity 24–5, 31, 33–4

core business: and direction of activity 51, 58, 79; and quality of activity 28, 29; and quantity of activity 9, 10, 12, 22; and territory management 69

costs 2; training 35

creativity 199

'Customer Revolution Conference' 24, 35

customers: base and quantity of activity 7, 8, 9–11, 19–21; classifying 67–9; going out of business 21; listing 9–18; lost to competition 21–3; loyalty 20, 179–80; mix 2, 6; profiling 76–8; records, private 111–12; *see also* existing customer base days, number of selling 48–9, 52

decision-making 139–40, 145 decline of product 72–3

defensiveness 161

delivery, collection instead of 157

'delusions of adequacy' 98

development, plan of 5–6, 191, 192

diary systems 113–15; computerised 115–17

'digging for gold' 160

Digital Equipment Corporation viii

direction of activity vii, 5, 9, 47–82; *see also* territory management

discipline, personal, when working from home 124–6

discounts 154, 158–9; early settlement 156; retrospective 155

dissipation rate 20, 32

Eadie, Gerard 201

early settlement discounts 156

effectiveness 27; and efficiency, difference between viii

efficient working in field viii, 109–26; car as mobile office 109–11; computers 115–16, 120–22; customer records, private 111–12; diary systems 113–14; electronic mail 117; mobile telephones and alternatives 118–22; *see also* home, working from 80/20 rule 10, 29

electronic mail 117

emergency situations 54

enthusiasm on telephone 90

evaluation of return on time invested 75–6

excellence, striving for 198

Exclusive Cleaning Group 84–5

existing customer base: and direction of activity 51, 54, 57, 58, 79; and quality of activity 28, 29, 33, 36, 38–41; and quantity of activity 9, 10, 12–13, 15,

22–3; *see also* core business;
infrequent buyers; regular
buying customers
extended payment terms 156

face to face, getting viii–ix,
83–108; cold calling 83–7;
see also telephone calls
failure to sell 25–7
fall back positions 128, 132
farmers 70–71
field sales *see* selling
financial targets 51, 55–6
financial turnover 6
five-week plan in territory
management 63–7
flow of business MAP 17–19
flow chart 5–6
forecasts 1–2
Fort, Lord 200
Fullarton, A & W 36
future: mortgaging 42–4;
results, backward planning
to ensure 28–35; securing
see consolidating position

geographical territory
management 57–67; 'clover
leaf' principle 57–63;
rolling five-week plan 63–7
goals *see* targets
Greenwood, Nigel 172–3
groups, selling to ix, 133–45;
at group call 137–40; before
group call 134–7; getting
decision 145; presentation
to 135–6, 137–8, 142–5;
tactics between meetings
141–2
growth of product 72–3

haggling 154; *see also*
discounts happiness 197

hi-tech solutions ix
home, working from ix,
122–6; isolation 123–4;
organisation and personal
discipline 124–6
hunters 70–71

information gathering 130
infrequent buyers: and
quality of activity 90; and
quantity of activity 9, 10,
13; and telephone calls 99
insurance company 34, 106–7,
181–2
interest 'grabber' 99
interrupting 144
introduction of product 72–3
isolation when working from
home 123–4

Just in Time supply 157–8

key account situation 134
KISS principle ('Keep It
Simple, Stupid') ix; call
reporting system 78–81
knowledge areas in personal
and career development
184, 185–6
known market 9
Kotler, Philip: *Marketing
Management* 74

Lansbury Hotels 172–3
last year's research, analysis
of 6
leasing companies 21
letters and proposals 174–8
life cycles *see* product life
cycles
listening 161
listing customers 9–18
lobbying 141

'locking in' activities 23
loyalty, customer 20, 179–80

Macfarlane, Lord and
 Macfarlane Group 36
mail, electronic 117
MAN (Money, Authority,
 Need) 93, 139–40
manager's presence 146–51;
 before call discussion
 147–9; reason for 147
manager's supplement in
 personal and career
 development 184, 189, 193
Managing Activity and
 Productivity (MAP) *see*
 business MAP
mapping the business viii;
 benefits of 44–6;
 significance of 41–2
market opportunities 9; and
 direction of activity 51, 52,
 54, 58; and quality of
 activity 24–5, 31; and
 quantity of activity 7–8, 18;
 and telephone calls 99
market research and quantity
 of activity 2–4, 6, 17
maturity of product 72–3
meaningful selling call 39–41
measurement *see* quality of
 activity
mobile office, car as 109–11
mobile telephones and
 alternatives 118–22
Money, Authority, Need *see*
 MAN
mortgaging future 42–4
multi-level contact 69, 179–80
multiple-call sale 131
Munro, Frank xi
'Murphy's Law' 54

naturalness on telephone 90-91
negotiation ix, 153–68; with
 authority 158–66; backing
 out of corner 166, 167–8;
 responsibility without
 authority 153–3; 'rules' 162;
 see also weakness new
 product 100
new targets, setting 4
number of calls: per day
 60–62, 64–7; per year 50
number of selling days 48–9,
 52

objections 132; overcoming
 101–5
objectives *see* targets
open questions 160–61, 163,
 164–5
opening gambit 154
opportunities *see* market
 opportunities; working
 opportunities
organisation, personal, when
 working from home 124–6

patience x
payment terms, extended 156
personal and career
 development ix, 35, 184–202
Peters, Tom 24, 35
planning 5–6; activity 44, 51,
 56, 58; backward to ensure
 future results 28–35;
 development 5–6, 191, 192;
 five-week in territory
 management 63–6; pre-call
 127–31, 134–7, 147–9; *see
 also* action plan
'poker faces' 164
policy decisions 4, 6
polite telephoning 93–4
Porter, Michael E.:
 Competitive Strategy 74

post-call analysis 131–3, 150–51

potential annual turnover, classification by 67–8

pre-call planning 127–31, 134–7, 147–9

preferrals 34, 180–83

presentation to groups 135–6, 137–8, 142–5

prices: and failure to sell 26–7; in letters and proposals 177; and negotiation 155; *see also* discounts priorities, setting 75–6

probability of success 36–9

product mix 2, 6; life cycles and territory management 69, 71–4; training 31

profiling customers and prospects 76–8

profitability 6

progressing existing customer base 38–41

proposals 174–8

prospects, profiling 76–8

psychology of success 193–202; self-analysis 196–7; ten-point plan for 198–200

purpose *see* targets

qualifications: analysis of 6; of sales people 5

quality of activity, measurement of vii, 5, 9, 24–46, 56; backward planning to ensure future results 28–35; and direction of activity 56, 58; mapping the business 41–2, 44–6; mortgaging future 42–4; progressing existing

customer base 38–41; success, probability of 36–8; working opportunities 38

quantity of activity vii, 1–23, 56; business MAP 7; customer base 9–11, 19–21; customers going out of business 21; customers lost to competition 21–3; and direction of activity 56, 79; steps in securing sales results 2–6; targets, budgets and forecasts 1–2; flow of business MAP 17–19; market opportunities 7–8; working opportunities 8–9

Radio Clyde 72

Rank Xerox 72, 87–8

reasons for purchases, real 77–8

receptionists and secretaries, problems with 91, 93–8

recording development plan 191, 192

referrals 34, 180–83

regular buying customers: and direction of activity 51, 54, 58, 79; and quality of activity 29, 33; and quantity of activity 9, 10, 15, 22–3; and telephone calls 100; and territory management 70–80

responsibility: for success 199; without authority 153–4

results, steps in securing sales 2–6

retrospective discounts 155

return on time invested, evaluation of 75–6